JOHN MacKENNA was born in 1952 in
Castledermot, County Kildare. His books include
The Fallen and Other Stories (1992), which won
The Irish Times First Fiction Award, *A Year of Our
Lives* (London, Picador, 1995) and *The Last Fine
Summer* (London, Picador, 1998).

things you should know

things you should know

JOHN MacKENNA

NEW ISLAND

Things You Should Know
First published 2006
by New Island
2 Brookside
Dundrum Road
Dublin 14

www.newisland.ie

isbn 1 905494 17 3

British Library Cataloguing in Publication Data.
A CIP catalogue record for this book is available
from the British Library.

Book design by New Island
Printed in Ireland by ColourBooks

10 9 8 7 6 5 4 3 2 1

*For Lydia and Ewan, with love
and in memory of my brother Jarlath*

prologue

John is working in the garden when his father comes looking for him. The light is beginning to quieten in the late afternoon. Beside him, a half-empty potato sack spills its seeds across the shining earth. The air smells of manure and growth, the hedges promise spring.

'Isn't it a bit early to be putting in spuds?' his father asks.

John goes on digging, turning the clay out of the drill.

'There'll be no growth, it's too cold.'

His father has been dead for five weeks and, yet, he isn't surprised by the voice at his shoulder. He turns out another mound of clay and then leans on the handle of his spade and looks along the drill. Sweat drips from his armpits and rivers down his back and legs, not from fear but from labour. His jacket hangs on a fence post. A light breeze touches one arm of the jacket and it waves shyly.

'And the drills are crooked,' his father says. 'You should have used a line.'

'I did.'

'Well the twine must be bent then.'

John smiles.

His father made the straightest drills himself. Once the soil was dug and turned and clear of weeds, he'd go into the shed and take down the line from the box on the top shelf. Two bits of stick with thirty feet of twine wrapped round them, there from year to year. And once he had the first drill lined up he'd turn the soil like a plough, his spade gliding through the rich clay, cutting, scooping, turning, building a bank beside the trench, forking in the manure, setting the potatoes and turning the drill back on itself.

John would leave home on spring evenings while his father was in the garden, digging, and wake the next morning to see deep, straight drills glistening in the early sun. He envied his father that skill, he still does. Maybe his father is right, maybe there is a bend on the twine.

'Why are they going in so early?'

'To beat the blight at the other end.'

'I'm telling you, there'll be no growth till the latter end of March. Let the last hour be the hardest.'

'So you say. Said.'

His father laughs.

'Have you anything else in?'

John shakes his head.

'That itself. And how are things?'

'All right.'

'The brighter days are coming.'

John nods.

'I always liked the spring.'

'They're promising a good summer.'

'I wouldn't put any store in that old stuff: *when the swallows fly upside down and backwards in May you'll have a white Christmas*. Bloody old nonsense.'

'How are things with you?'

'Never better. You've no need to worry about me.'

'Good.'

The breeze lifts again and the pale sun goes out. Almost immediately sleet begins to fall.

'Get in out of that, you'll get your death. And put on that coat of yours. It'll do you no good hanging there on the post.'

John nods and steps across the drill.

'I'll see you,' his father says and John doesn't question him because he knows by his father's tone that he will.

Instead, pulling on his jacket, he gathers the fallen seeds into the sack and humps it into the shelter of the shed. Sleet clatters the corrugated-iron roof and whitens the top of the orchard and, for no better reason than that it comes into his head, he imagines his father, a small boy, trudging home from school, caught in the falling snow at the Carlow Road crossing-gates.

one

A glorious evening, the first week of the hay-golden August of 1992. The windows open. The children chattering and laughing on the back seat, a hot wind sweeping through the car.

John and his family are driving to see a cottage. He and his wife have told the children he hopes to rent it as a writing retreat. It's on the edge of Mullaghcreelan Wood, one of their favourite places, just a couple of miles from where his father lives. Already the children are making plans.

'I might not get it,' he warns but they're not having any of it.

'Can we stay out here when you're not too busy?'

'I haven't got it yet.'

'Yeah but when you do.'

'Let's just wait and see,' his wife says.

A big red sun is hanging to their right, high above the Barrow Valley, and John is thinking of the only other time he's ever been inside the garden gate of the cottage. That was evening time, too, almost thirty years ago, and he was with his father who was a Labour Party candidate in the local elections. He has vague memories of immaculate flower and vegetable patches and box hedges. He remembers an elderly man in the garden, and a frail and graceful woman, the man's sister, at the door, and their politeness when he handed over the election literature, their assurances that they would *favour* his father with a vote. When was that? The early Sixties and he was ten years old.

A voice interrupts from the back seat.

'Will you have food in this house?'

'I told you, I haven't got it yet.'

'Well, if you do get it, will there be food in it?'

'Yes.'

'And drinks?'

'Yes.'

'Will you have a TV?'

'I don't know.'

'I think you should have a TV there because if you get tired writing and you want to take a break and it's raining outside and you can't go out you could sit down and watch the TV for a while.'

'Right.'

He's trying to be calm. He wants the children to shut up, to leave him with his thoughts. He wonders what his wife is thinking.

They're at the top of the hill, a hundred yards from the cottage and he's nervous. He really wants to get this place. He wants it to work out. Perhaps he should have come alone.

'Are we nearly there?'

'We must be nearly there.'

'For God's sake, can you both not just be quiet.'

'They're all right.'

They pass the old green roadside pump and there's the cottage, low against the yellow fields. He turns off the road, down a short dusty track that leads to the distant farmyard and then swings immediately left into the gateway of the cottage. Its windows are open and the evening heat stretches lazily across the overgrown garden.

The owner steps from the doorway and comes to welcome them. She takes them on a tour of the house. They talk about the benefits of having a space in which to write. They talk about peace and quiet. They talk about how the children would love coming out here at week-ends. They talk about the attractions of country life. They talk about money and, suddenly, the cottage is John's, at a much lower rent than he'd expected, and it's agreed that he will move his typewriter and books in at the end of the week.

'I'll leave you to have a look around,' the owner says. 'I hope you'll be happy and productive here.'

They move again through the six empty rooms – scullery, kitchen, hallway, bathroom, bedroom and sitting room. The cottage is everything he wants, small and spartan, in the heart of the country and on the edge of the woods. Overlooked by hundred-year-old trees, overlooking the rich, swelling fields of south Kildare.

'Which room will you put your typewriter in?'

'This one.'

'Why?'

'Because it has a fireplace.'

'The other room has a fireplace, too.'

'This one is brighter in the evening time. That'll be the bedroom.'

'Will you have a bedroom here?'

'Yes. For when I'm working late.'

'What's the big fire in the kitchen for?'

'It's an Aga range. You can cook on it.'

'But there's a gas cooker there too.'

'Well, we'll have a choice, then, won't we?'

And off the children go.

He leans through the open sitting-room window, taking the heat of the falling sun. The children race around outside the cottage, investigating the garage and the empty pigsty behind it. His wife stands in the gateway, watching them.

They drive back along the road they travelled earlier, back home. The sun has set but the sky is still a deep and vivid blue, soaked with the promise of another scorching day. The children are chatter-full of plans for hideouts in the garage, for adventures up Mullaghcreelan Hill, for family picnics in the garden, for having their friends come and stay in this new and enticing retreat. His wife is silent. And he is what? Apprehensive, excited, terrified, impatient, stunned that, suddenly, the cottage is his for at least a year. Possibility opens before him.

Here he is, a writer who has just rented a place in which to write his first novel.

Here they are, a family going home from an evening in the country. He thinks of those childhood schoolbooks that show happy families doing happy family things. *Here is mother. Here is father. Here is daughter. Here is son. See them drive. See the family in the sunshine. See them laugh. They are going home. They have a dog that is waiting for them. His name is Nash. He will run and wag his tail when he sees them come.*

He moves into the cottage in the late summer. It's a plain, single-storey, granite house, built on the edge of the wood on the road between Castledermot and Athy. He will learn that on damp days it will soak up the rain and weep. In spring it will only slowly give up the dampness it has sponged up through the winter months. But on these late summer days it keeps its coolness, even when the weather is hot and dry and still.

It's a strange and painful time for John and his family. And, although the children don't know the real reason for his going, the life they've taken for granted is changing, allowing him to step back into independence after fifteen years of married life. There's a strangeness, too, in the fact that the cottage is no more than three miles from the village where he was born and grew up, a place where he wanted to but never truly belonged.

When the moment comes, he realises that no talk and no rehearsal can prepare for this. When his typewriter and books and stereo have been put carefully in the car, when the children have finished checking that everything is in place, when they stand with his wife to wave him off on what they believe is an adventure, there is a suddenness he had not expected. Suddenly he's leaving his family, his way of life, the stability of the familiar, the comfort of friends. And he's bringing with him a gnawing sensation of failure and betrayal, though the word sensation can never do justice to the depth and pain of those feelings.

That first evening in the cottage is a warm one, evidence of an Indian summer still to come. Once the car is unloaded, he unpacks and arranges some of his books in the room he'll use as a study.

He sits over the books, their magic smell lifting from the cardboard boxes. He opens paperbacks he bought in the Seventies. He finds a London underground map, two tickets for the Royal Albert Hall, dated Saturday, July 19 1975, scribbled phone numbers and underlined passages.

He moves his little table and the heavy manual type-writer from place to place, trying to find a natural home for them – at the window, in the corner, in the centre of the room. Finally, he settles on a space near the fireplace. He doesn't turn on the lamps; instead the light outside softens to a rich honey that leaks into the house and tints everything. The night is beautiful and frightening, full of promise, yet filled with solitude. He stands in the last light and he's not thinking about books or words or stories. He's thinking about his children. He imagines them saying their prayers and climbing into bed. He's thinking how wonderful it would be if he were here just to write, if this were just an adventure.

The following morning he stands in the middle of this room, unable and unwilling to work. He is ashamed, sorrowful, self-pitying, lonely, hopeless, desperate, lost and terrified. Last evening's sun has run like a gentle dye from September into this first day of October but there's a darkness inside him that's oblivious, and he feels isolated and despondent. Life can never be the same again, can never be as good or as complete or as hope-filled as it was. And, yet, in spite of everything, he has a cold, hard understanding that there's no going back, no undoing what has been done, no hope or fear of reconciliation.

He knows that what's unfolding isn't, in any sense, an unusual story; there's little new about it, but it's new to him and new to his wife and new to his children.

He knows that the end of love and the end of a marriage rarely taper neatly. Often, the union is over but love refuses to accept failure and, often, the love is gone but the partnership continues. As with all emotions – to begin is not necessarily to end, nor is an end inevitably a beginning.

He lies awake, hearing the new sounds of an old house, believing that sadness will inevitably wrap itself around the children. And, in that fog of betrayal and loss and hesitancy, he will lean on them more than he can ever support them. He needs them more than they need him. He has chosen not to live with them but he can't live without them. He wants their nights and weekends together to be happy but he feels himself drifting into a state where he's in no condition to attempt anything even closely akin to happiness. He lives in fear of what he knows to be around the corner.

He thinks about his wife. He remembers the night they met. He drove past this cottage on his way to the dance where he first saw her. She told him she lived on the canal and he believed her. Only when he left her home did he discover that her house was on the banks of the canal, rather than on the water itself. They spent the hours after that dance sitting in her kitchen, drinking coffee, talking, discovering they shared the same birth date, half-heartedly arguing the merits and demerits of Van Gogh and Picasso. And at five o'clock the following morning, as day was threatening to break, he drove back past this cottage. If he had known then what he knows now.

He longs for the impossible – for second chances, for the unwinding of clocks, for the comfort of hindsight. And he longs for their children and for a clean way back or a painless way out. But he longs, too, for things that are more mundane.

He misses their dog. He misses the familiar walks he took with him down the riverbank. He misses his desk. He misses the wall of books in his study. He misses the rich dark smell of stock in the yard. He misses the kitchen window filled with laburnum. He misses the small back garden. He misses the nuisances that were also consolations, the constant, mild annoyance of the stream of visitors to the house. He misses the sound of children playing in the street. He misses the sound of a phone ringing.

Comfort becomes a primary word in his life. In the times when he is most self-centred, most sorry for himself, he regrets the loss of comfort. He adopts a mantle of martyrdom. He has to remind himself that he chose to leave all that solace behind and deliberately stepped into the harsh world of self-reliance and a new beginning. Austerity is the watchword.

In spite of all this, in these early days, this freedom, this living apart, is sometimes a game. John tells himself that he's not playing at being alone. He consoles himself with the thought that this is a trial and *they'll see how it goes*.

As autumn advances, the cottage breathes deeply, taking great, gulping sucks of rain and cloud back into its walls. Yet the insatiable thirst in its granite skin is matched by an aura of safekeeping and refuge. Coming home to the cottage feels like truly coming home. Even on the darkest nights and in the harshest gales, when the wind whips low across the stubbled fields from Maganey and Levitstown, hitting the cottage before battering the woods above it, there's always a feeling of welcome in the dark pantry. And there's always a glimmer among the ashes in the old range. And, once the fire is going and the curtains are drawn against the night outside, the house settles itself contentedly and whispers its own hushed language of welcome, of gladness that someone is home.

He doesn't flatter himself that it matters greatly who that someone is, but he does recognise in it a need for people, a softening at their arrival, a warming to them, a holding of them to its heart. It's a house that is gracious and generous. And not every house is as welcoming. He has stepped inside doors and known, intuitively, that a house is unfriendly.

He tries to be positive. Moving here is a step away from things and a step closer to things. Away from the past, the pain, the uncertainty, the unhappiness he created, closer to other parts of his life, to several kinds of history. Closer, too, to self-reliance, nature, the joy of solitude.

He sets off on a long evening walk, down Mullaghcreelan Hill to Kilkea Bridge, the most beautiful road he has ever walked, a road he travelled, twice daily, as a child with his father. A road that's dressed in crab-apple blossom in the spring and bends, now, with the fruit of autumn branches.

He walks in the shadow of the trees, down to the foot of the hill and along to the bridge. He fully expects something mystical from this walk, something more carnal than the beauty of the late August countryside. He has a sudden, acute anticipation that this road will provide him with some human contact, an encounter of consequence. But it doesn't. Instead, all the possibilities that it promised in his boyhood and adolescence evaporate. He walks the road but he meets hardly anyone and, when he does, they cycle past with a nod or a word and are gone about their business. And why shouldn't they? If they know him at all they probably assume he's here for a ramble, out from the town for an hour.

Another evening. He sits on the bridge and listens to the water of the Griese, slipping and pittering across the rocks beneath the arches and wonders whether the return journey will prove any more stimulating. It doesn't. A week into the routine, it's dawning on him that no one is waiting out here to befriend him.

He continues the evening walks but, now, for the exercise rather than in anticipation. He consoles himself with the thought that the beauty of the landscape is more important than the figures who cross it. The year is poised on a leaf, to be savoured before the fall. The fields have sucked a deep, rich golden from the sun but the hedges are still staunch against the knife of winter.

This, he tells himself, is what he wanted, this is one of the reasons why he was so anxious to live here. This is the life for a writer. This is real independence and, given time, it will produce the books he wants to write and the freedom he needs to write them.

He tells himself many things but his heart refuses to believe them.

two

It's a long time ago and I'm sitting in the kitchen of a house on the Low Terrace on a cold, wet evening. The wind is lifting in from the east, banging the back door, holding the winter over us like a threat. The kitchen table is set for tea, crowded with mugs and plates and knives. There's a big pat of butter in the middle. One of the girls of the house sits at the open range, toasting bread on two long toasting forks. As each slice is toasted on one side, she turns it over and toasts it on the other. I sit and watch, astonished at her patience, at the gradual growing evenness of the golden brown she gets on every slice. That much done, she places the toast on a huge plate that sits to the side of the range.

Suddenly, the back door opens and the girl's father is blown in on the whistling lips of the gale. His coat is saturated with rain and his trousers are plastered against his legs. He shakes himself in the scullery and kicks off his boots.

'Go and change into your Sunday clothes,' his wife says, 'the supper is near ready.'

My mother calls our evening meal *tea* but everyone else on the Terrace calls it supper.

The man passes through the kitchen, winking at me.

'Good man.'

Ten minutes later he's back, wearing the trousers of his Sunday suit, the only other clothes he owns. He carries the soaking work trousers, shirt and coat and hangs them on the sheila above the range. In seconds the steam begins to rise. He goes back into the scullery and I hear a tap running. When he returns, he's carrying his boots, stuffed with newspaper and he puts them between the legs of the range.

'Will we ate then?'

We gather round the table – the man, his wife, his children and me, the neighbours' child from up the road. The woman sets a steaming plate of rashers, sausages, eggs, puddings and fried potatoes before the man. The rest of the family ate dinner at midday. We sit and butter our toast and drink our tea.

'Well, how was school?'

'It was good.'

'It was all right.'

'We got drenched coming home.'

'Did yis not run between the drops? I used to run between the drops and I comin' home from school.'

We laugh.

'Was this man's mother hard on yis?'

Now he's laughing.

'Did you know, she was my first teacher?'

I shake my head.

'She was begor.'

We finish our food and clear the table. I see my friend's father start to rise from his seat but then the energy goes out of him and he sits back down and lays his head on his folded arms and closes his eyes.

'Forty winks,' he says, quietly.

I notice the clay of the day's work, still streaked high across his forehead. I see the cuts and gouges on the backs of his hands. I hear the depth of his breath as he draws it in and lets it out.

When I leave for home, an hour later, he's still asleep at the table, like one of the infants in school at rest time.

three

It's a dark evening and the scarf of fields around the wood lights up the sky. He stands on the doorstep and breathes in the smell of hot clay and burning stubble. A week from now, the fields will turn from black to chestnut as the ploughmen go steadily about their work. And then a day of rain and the fields will become a more solid, settled mahogany and, when the rain eases off, John will walk out of the shelter of the woods and onto the long sloping field that has kept the scattered, harrowed ruins of a fallen cottage for a generation.

Each year this field has been ploughed and each disturbance has turned up some new treasure. On dry afternoons, when he's not working, he walks a section of the field, head bent, eyes straining for a glimpse of some connection with the people who lived on this hillside before him. While he's out here walking, being the historian he trained to be, nothing else impinges on his life. He works the field meticulously, knowing he could stay here all his life and still find artefacts that are new to him. He tells himself he's putting together something of the people whose names and faces he doesn't even know. He tries to ignore the fact that while he's here, he doesn't have to concern himself with the desperation of his own life.

He spreads newspapers on the kitchen table and removes the caked clay, carefully washing the bits and pieces he has found. And the treasures become clearer. The bowl of a clay pipe, stamped *Ben Nevis Cutty*; a carbide lamp; an earthen jam pot; Corcoran's lemonade bottles.

The windowsill in the garage fills with shards of pottery and odds and ends of broken machinery carried home from the field. John remembers how his wife used to sigh, benignly, and ask why he was cluttering their house with the remnants he brought back from long walks with the dog?

He's drifting through these early weeks of October, trying to ignore the gloom that's closing around him. Blocking out the fact that this time he has to deal with the seasonal rats in his head. There's no one to talk to, no voice saying: 'It's not that bad. If we did this or that ….' The word *we* has dropped out of his vocabulary, leaving only the ghost-memories of courtship and the promises made and the promise drawn from those days.

The first early summer day when they crossed the hill above this house and stumbled into the acres of scent and colour that were to become *the bluebell wood* on the remote side of Mullaghcreelan. It was an afternoon in late May and the summer sun had come with an unexpected ferocity that drew the fragrance from the waves of blue petals washing the roots of the old sycamore and beech and ash trees. The forest was thick with birdsong and, immediately, foggy with a blue light and a fragrance that he had never caught before. They had stepped into the perfection of love reflected. Nature was throwing its carpet before their feet, the world reminding them that they were young and that there was much that was new for them and much that was beautiful and that life could fulfil every promise they had made to each other. They were looking through the open gates of paradise and no one was rushing to close them.

They carried arms of bluebells home that evening and, the following afternoon, John went back when school was finished, and walked out into the sea of flowers and breathed deeply and watched the breeze swelling across the hillside, brushing flower against flower, and promising luck and beauty and love and hope and the possibility that was *us*.

It's Saturday. He turns at the foot of the long sloping field and looks back up the hundreds of yards to the apron of Mullaghcreelan Wood and knows that he can't stay here forever. He can't spend his life uncovering the buried cast-offs of other people's lives. He can't live in memory.

The weather is settling and the cottage is resuming its habit of sucking rain from the grey skies that close in low above it. John has taken to walking in the woods, in the shelter of the trees. He now knows where the badgers have their setts. He has discovered the routes the bats sweep at dusk.

It's late afternoon and he's skirting along the edge of the wood, on a ditch that rises high above the passing road. He's paralysed by the sight of a young fox gambolling in a patch of fragile sunlight that kisses the tar below him. The animal rolls and chases his tail, his rich red coat surging and splashing at every turn. And then he rolls again, barking and twisting, scratching his back on the warm, hard road. And so he continues until the sound of an oncoming car frightens him and, instantly, he's a solitary Bolshevik disappearing across the ruin of a stubbled field. John watches him until there's nothing left to watch and then stumbles home exhilarated.

He decorates the house. He buys nuts and balloons and sweets and biscuits. He bakes two apple tarts. He makes sandwiches. He gathers dead wood from the forest and builds an enormous bonfire in the back garden.

Halloween night is mild and dry. Flames light the dark sky. Sparks fly up to join the stars. People are singing. There's food and drink and games. There's a lot of laughter. The children are in their element, running breathlessly about the place, showing their friends the nooks and crannies of the house and the garden.

'Are you enjoying yourself?'

'Yes, thank you.'

'Good. Another drink?'

'No, thank you. We won't be staying long.'

'Ah, right. Well enjoy yourself while you do.'

'I just want to tell you, I don't think this is a good idea. What you're doing.'

'The party?'

'Not the party – as you well know. It's a dangerous game. What you're doing is irresponsible.'

The woman steps away and the firelight is angry in her eyes.

'You were happy. Why would you want to break that happiness? Once you break it, it's broken for everyone. Especially your children.'

Towards ten, as the fire is dying, he leads an excursion up the hill. A few well-placed surprises, skulls with candles inside, ghost sheets on swinging branches, come out of the darkness as his flashlight conveniently fails. He's almost lured into believing things are normal.

And now, afterwards, and it seems there will always be an afterwards, there's the silence. He sits on an upturned box in the garden and watches the last of the smouldering flames blow away. He reminds himself that this is what he wanted. This is independence. But an answer comes back from somewhere that no, this isn't it at all.

He imagines the woman's voice and other voices.

'Well, if reclusive is what he wants then, by God, reclusive is what he'll get.'

'Anyway, it's not as if we were *his* friends in the first place.'

'Writer! I know the kind of writing he's interested in.'

'He'll be dipping more than his pen out there!'

The more he wrestles with the whole thing the more irrational he becomes. He sifts through the names of friends and separates the ones he imagines will continue their friendship from those that won't.

'Irresponsible,' the woman said.

She may see it like that but, of all the things he's ever been, irresponsible isn't one, not for as long as he can remember – not since childhood. Teetotal, non-smoking, buggy-pushing, caught-in-the-middle, he's been all those things, still is inside his head. But irresponsible? Not in his mind or heart or soul, not then and not now. And he doubts he'll ever have the choice.

He smiles a wry smile. A hectic, laughing Halloween night melts into a dismal, reflective dawn.

four

Once again, I'm standing at our kitchen window, looking down the length of the empty road. It's late afternoon, the end of a long, grey day. There hasn't been a stab of sunshine for over a week. No one is out playing and the road is wet and it looks like it's going to rain again. And then I see him *traipsing* up the Low Terrace. Traipsing is a word my mother uses and I think it fits the way he shuffles, without lifting his feet from the ground. His back is bent, the way it always is. He looks like a skeleton with a thin, dirty overcoat pinned against the wind. I watch him for a while and then I shout the news to my mother.

'Jack-the-Basket-Man is coming. He's leaving Byrne's now. He's going into Condron's but there's no one there, I saw them going out a while ago.'

But the Basket-Man doesn't know this, so I watch him shuffling his low, heavy shuffle up the pathway. I see him knock on Condron's door. He waits. He doesn't knock a second time. He never knocks a second time. That's how he is. If people aren't in or people don't want to open the door to him he won't push into their lives. Instead, he shambles back along the path and carefully closes the gate behind him, moving on to the next house. His basket hangs from his arm; it doesn't swing the way I see baskets swinging on women's arms downtown. His eyes are on the ground. On he comes. Whelan's, Howe's, Kinsella's, Behan's, Whelan's-next-door and our house.

'Away from the window, don't stare,' my mother warns and I drop the corner of the curtain and wait for his knock.

When my mother opens the door, my sister and I stand behind her and inspect the old man's torn coat and shabby hat while she roots a coin from her purse and the basket-man hands over a printed prayer and a flower made from old sweet wrappers. No one speaks.

No sooner has he left our doorstep than flower and prayer are thrown into the lighted range. My mother mutters something about TB.

'Charity or not,' she says, 'there's no sense in taking chances.'

Jack-the-Basket-Man lives on a side road near the Turnpike. Some people call it Basket Lane. His home is a hole in the ground, a trench covered by a sheet of galvanised iron, the door is another sheet laid against the roof.

Sometimes, when summer takes us to that part of the village, we dare each other to look inside. Someone swears they saw the Basket-Man go off selling his flowers and prayers. Someone faces someone on the dusty side road and says, 'You're afraid of your shite.' But, in the end, someone's courage always fails at the door and we content ourselves with throwing stones against the galvanised roof, half-expecting the noise to bring him shuffling after us. It never does, so we give up. We're bored and, anyway, he probably isn't there at all, and we all troop off to Mullarney in search of courting couples.

One summer evening, I overhear my father talking to a local Guard. They mention Jack-the-Basket-Man and my ears prick up.

'Sometimes he stays in there for days on end, just lying in the trench. It must be a killer to lie there in the dark, in this heat, and to be afraid to come out.'

Afterwards, I ask my father about him.

'They say he was in the British Army during the First War. He's harmless but he's probably shell-shocked.'

It's Saturday and the sun is lifting the tar off the roads in big blisters. I'm on the Turnpike with a couple of the Terrace lads. We go down to the corner where Jack has his trench. Maybe he's in there, hiding in the sweaty dimness under his iron roof. Maybe he's hiding from us, from our voices, from our pretend hand-grenades. Maybe the crash when the stones land on the roof above him reminds him of the war. Maybe he is afraid.

'Fuck him, he's a mad old bastard and he's riddled with the pox.'

I don't know what the pox is and I don't ask and I don't disagree because now I'm afraid that if I do my friends will turn on me and say I have it, too.

five

November arrives, cold, sharp, rainy. Even in the over-hang of the beeches the forest floor is soaked and churned wherever he walks. The leaves have fallen and the trees that were impressive in the breadth of their spread and shelter are empty frames propping the sky.

Apart from his day-job in a radio station, John is working on the first draft of a novel about the English poet John Clare, seen through the eyes of the women in his life, a life that smells of wet timber and rain and ditches. He spends part of each day living in that past, trying to do some of the things Clare did, gathering timber from the wood, walking the fields, sitting and listening to the voices of nature. And listening for the voices of the women. Everywhere he goes, he takes a small tape-recorder and when lines, ideas, conversations come into his head he records them.

On the days when he doesn't have to drive into Dublin for work, he takes a morning walk and gathers enough timber to feed the fires for the day. He piles it, dripping, beside the range and it spits and sizzles when he throws it on its bed of coal. The rooms have a strange and permanent smell of burning wetness, a smell from the houses of his schooldays.

He thinks of the evenings, after school in Athy, when his father was late collecting him from his uncle's shop. He's back there again. Walking up Leinster St, he sees the Morris Minor outside Clancy's pub and stands on the footpath, willing his father to come out, knowing what lies ahead at home, arguments, silences. The pub door opens, someone is leaving. He steps forward and glimpses his father perched on a stool. The door swings closed again. He feels a hand on his shoulder. Another of the railwaymen has seen him and guides him into the bar.

'And who's this?' someone asks.

'Oh, this is the youngest, the shake of the bag,' his father says, laughing. He's in good humour and he asks Mrs Clancy to give John *a bottle of minerals*.

Or he's in a bad humour and his tone is sharp as a barber's shop.

'Isn't it very hard to get a bit of peace or ease for yourself.'

Grudgingly, a bottle of lemonade is ordered but John is left swinging his feet on one of the benches.

Or he thinks of the spring and summer evenings when his father is anxious to be home and out to the garden.

And then he thinks about his own children and the comfort and enjoyment that's such a part of their lives. And he tells himself they're lucky. Yet, what does he know of their feelings? He's not there when they come home in the evenings and, most mornings, he's not there to take them to school. He sees them almost every day but he can't truly claim to be part of their lives. He has no right to make any assumptions.

'How long will it take you to finish this book?' his son asks.

'A while.'

They're sitting at the table in the cottage. It's a dismal Saturday afternoon and they've had to abandon their walk up the hill.

'Why don't you write this book in your study at home, like you did the last one?'

'This one's different. I need to have more time and quietness.'

'You're away a long time, aren't you?'

'I suppose I am.'

His daughter says nothing. John glances at her and sees something in her eye that says: 'You're full of crap.'

But he's only been gone ten weeks, how could she even begin to suspect that his present circumstance has already become their permanent condition? Can intuition begin so early in a young girl's life? He tells himself not.

'I know it's taking a long time but it'll be worth it in the end.'

'Will you be rich and famous when it's finished?'

'I doubt it but maybe. If we're lucky.'

And there's that look again.

He's in the local supermarket, where he meets a woman he's known since childhood and they get talking and he thinks about inviting her to drop into the cottage if she's passing but he doesn't.

The winter is closing in and he's becoming reclusive. Even when the children come to stay, he can't muster the energy to do things with them. They go for walks up the woods, when the weather allows, but rarely do anything else.

'There's a good film on in Carlow,' his daughter says. 'Mam took us to it last night.'

'You should have told me about it, we could have gone today. It doesn't always have to be with Mary, you just have to say.'

'I did, last Saturday.'

'Did you?'

'Yeah, remember, I said Dee had seen it.'

'Oh, well, tell me next time.'

'Yeah right,' comes out as a deep sigh.

'And don't be smart!'

He doesn't think of himself as depressed. He doesn't feel depressed; he has energy for work and energy for writing and energy for exercise but he has no energy for engaging with people. He tries to dismiss it as the resurrection of his old shyness, opting for loneliness in the guise of privacy.

He recognises the irony in his being stuck for a voice. He remembers a girlfriend from his college days. When they were together, when they had time and opportunity and need, he stumbled and stuttered his way through her affections and his longing, rarely finding a way to say what he wanted to say.

He wonders about whether it really mattered, whether they were good at talking or not? Would it have made a difference if conversation had come more easily to him? He remembers telling that girlfriend, years after they'd uncovered the truths about each other, that he'd make lists when he was going to Dublin to see her. He must have had a dozen of those lists in the car at one time or another. Had he had the courage to be himself, they might have known each other truly, seen each other as they really were and had so much more time together.

He had carried a perpetual fear that the girl didn't care, but she cared an awful lot.

In his marriage it had been different: there had been someone to depend on. His wife was good at socialising, she organised dinners and parties and the like. Now there's no one to do that and it's a skill he doesn't have.

He sets himself the task of tracing information on the life of Jack-the-Basket-Man. He contacts the British Army and verifies the Basket-Man's real name and his regiment and, sure enough, there he is. A man with a past, discharged in shock, a man with a name. Jack Fitzgerald. Jack-the-Basket-Man.

It's a murky afternoon, he drives to Castledermot and sits in a pew near the back of the Catholic Church. He's reminded of the neighbours' house on the Low Terrace and that wintry night when he sat at the kitchen table with the family and ate toast. He thinks of the father of that family who died not long afterwards. He thinks of the things that the man's children told him later, things they wouldn't have known as children. He knows they were left with the memory of a father exhausted and asleep at the table forever. He knows the man cycled five miles to and from a job that started before sunrise and ended long after the sun had been washed over the waterfall at the end of the earth. He knows he earned a pittance. He remembers how the man and his wife kept a pin-clean home.

He watches the last drops of wet, grey light wrung through the stained-glass windows. Dusk begins to settle in the quiet nave. The red sanctuary lamp burns fierce and unwavering above the altar but the handful of candles before the statues jitter and falter each time the winter wind storms the old doors.

What is he looking for in here?

Peace? He has peace in the woods and fields.

Certainty? Certainty is something he has to go back a long way to find. It's been twenty-seven years since he regularly attended Mass in this church and even then he had doubts and a want for which he couldn't find a satisfactory solution. He didn't give up easily and here he is, again, not sure of what he left and not sure of where he's going and completely lost when it comes to where exactly he is.

He settles back, easy with the darkness and the emptiness and the stillness. He's used to churches, he likes them. His fondness has to do with history and the smells of candle smoke and wood and polish and the shadowy scent of incense. It has to do with empty choir galleries and the faint, almost perceptible reverberation of long-ago music. His faith, like his life, has depended on the comfort of the familiar. The Latin hymns.

He begins to hum but not so loudly that anyone might hear. The words come back, instilled in childhood.

'Tantum ergo sacramentum veneremur cernui:
Et antiquum documentum novo cedat ritui …'

And there are the words and lines of litanies.

'Jesus, Son of the living God,
Jesus, Splendour of the Father,
Jesus, Brightness of eternal light …
Jesus, most amiable,

Jesus, most admirable …
Jesus most patient,
Jesus, most obedient,
Jesus, Lover of chastity.'

And so it continues, a mantra whose recitation gives succour, without demanding consideration. It's all in there – life and light, the admirable and the amiable, patience and obedience. And chastity. Easy to say and, of late, easy to live. When did sex last cross his mind? He can't remember and he can't be bothered trying.

He can't find God and he can't find happiness and, for once, he has no one to blame but himself.

And, tonight, when he prays to the God whose existence he doubts, what will he do? Recite another litany, of the people he loves, alive and dead, and hope the mention of their names will remind that clouded deity of their lives and stir some kind of compassion. John's catalogue lengthens year by year, an extension ladder of names, summing up causes, lost and otherwise, for which he prays.

He hears a movement behind the altar. Probably the sacristan, come to close the church. He doesn't want to explain his presence here in the dark. He doesn't want to talk. He slips outside, gets into his car and drives.

six

Every afternoon, when my mother locks the girls' school door, I follow her down the street to the parish church, to make the Stations of the Cross. I'm in fourth class and I don't really like the Stations, the fourteen pictures that hang in heavy, dark frames on the church wall and tell the story of Jesus' last journey, from the time of his arrest to the time of his burial. They bore me because they never change. The centurion has that same look constantly on his face. Pilate never gets to wash his hands. Jesus' eyes are forever turned skywards as he hangs on the cross. Nothing changes, nothing happens.

In spring and early summer, the sunlight through the stained-glass windows makes big blots and looking down the nave of the church is like peering into a kaleidoscope. The pews are dipped and tie-dyed in water-coloured paints.

In winter, the rain runs down the outsides of the windows and I always expect one colour to leak into the next. The Jesus in the window weeps as the drops flow down his face, soaking his tunic, making puddles around his feet on the metal ledge between one colour and the next.

I always race ahead of my mother, finishing the Stations in half the time it takes her. Then, I sit near the back of the church, listening to the rain or watching the way the sunlight changes from pane to pane.

Most afternoons, Miss Crosby is there too, making her round of the Stations. She teaches in the school and is a friend of my mother's. I wait every afternoon, willing them to nod or smile as they pass each other but they never do. It's as if each is invisible to the other. Yet, when the Stations are done, they'll spend an hour talking outside but in here not a word.

What fascinates me even more than Miss Crosby is her handbag. It's a big, leather satchel that creaks each time she genuflects and creaks when she reaches inside to take out her rosary beads and creaks when she transfers it from one arm to the other. But, most of all, it creaks when, having finished her Stations, she goes to light her candles.

Standing at the shrine near the back of the nave, she opens the bag and dips inside, taking out two three-penny pieces, English three-penny pieces, sharp sided, gleaming golden in the candlelight. And then she places them slowly on the lip of the money drawer and pauses as each gently drops.

And, all the time, her bag sings its warm, comfortable, creaking song. This woman is *sophisticated*. At least, I think that's what she is. I've heard my mother say so. She's educated, well-off. She lives alone. She answers to no one.

I sit, half-turned, chin on the back of my hand, watching her. The noise of her bag is the most wonderful sound I have ever heard. I dream of a time when I, too, will have an endless trove of three-penny bits, when I can light as many candles as I want.

As an altar boy, I spend a lot of time in the church. Sunday Masses, Benediction, weddings, funerals, christenings are part of my life.

On Holy Saturday night I'll be there with the others, serving at midnight Mass for the first time. In the afternoon there's a practice, everything must be right, the curate is not a man to suffer mistakes.

On the way to the church I see a frog in the grass at Carlow Gate. I pick the animal up and put it in my trouser pocket.

It's a full dress rehearsal so we put on our surplices and soutanes and progress in pairs up the aisle; stand in our places; rehearse the responses; listen to the instructions and then do it all again. And again.

Then there's a lull while the curate goes to sign a Mass card. Sitting on the altar steps, I take the frog from my pocket and place it gently on the back of another boy's neck. The animal slides into the opening between the boy's shirt and his back. Silence and then a scream and the boy is dancing across the altar, struggling to free whatever it is that's hopping around inside his clothes. The surplice and soutane come off, his jumper and shirt are torn from his back and the frog escapes onto the altar. But the shouting has brought the curate running.

'What is going on,' he says and his voice is booming.

'There was something down my back, Father,' the shirtless boy stammers.

The curate spots the frog, staring up at him from the marble floor.

'Who is responsible for this?'

Silence.

'I am, Father.'

I know I'm in trouble.

'It was just a joke.'

'In God's house, on God's altar, on this day of all days. Take that creature and release it and then put your surplice and soutane in their place in the vestry and go home. You are suspended from altar service indefinitely.'

'Ah, Father …'

'Go. Now!'

I trudge home and tell my parents, expecting the worst.

'Me old *segocia*,' my father says, putting his arm around me. 'It's time that man took himself a bit less seriously. If that's the worst that ever happens, he'll be doing well.'

Seven

John is working seriously on his novel. Winter has made itself at home and his walks are taken in the teeth of wind and rain and sleet, under leafless trees and in the little shelter of stripped ditches which dig deep against the strength of the gales.

In the radio station, he spends his time wishing he were back at the cottage, writing. On the days when he is there, before he begins writing, he gathers wood on the hill, lumbering back down with his arms full of fallen, wet, green branches that soak his working coat and leave it smelling of moss and decay.

Once the fire is going, he settles down. The reek of damp timber and smoke brings him close to the soul of John Clare and he spends the mornings writing about the poet.

When he hits a blank, he pulls on his boots and coat and heads across the fields or up through the woods, Clare's poems and the tape-recorder in his pocket, in search of the poet's ghost. And Clare always puts in an appearance – sometimes distant, sometimes at his shoulder – and he comes home with words to write, a way of picking up what he left behind.

It's a misty December night. He climbs to the top of Mullaghcreelan Hill. He carries no flashlight. The fog has sucked enough light from the moon to brighten his way between the trees and out onto the open summit. The mist has cut off everything – sight and sound – leaving only perfect, heavy silence. No other world exists and this is how he wants it. He wants to know how John Clare felt when he walked the fens, long after night had fallen.

John takes off his clothes and stands in the swirling mist, letting the cold air trickle and drip across his skin. He is God and he is no one. He is everything and he is nothing. He is the world and he is isolation. He is free and he is a prisoner. He is himself and he is John Clare. He is waiting for a friend. Clare is waiting for his dead love, Mary Joyce. He is ecstatic, yet drained of every ounce of energy. This is what he wants, this closeness to the poet, this openness to the man. No price is too high to pay. He lets the night roll over him, allows the mist and the damp make love to him, feels every trickle of sweat and cold and hope and loss.

No one comes from the dead but he gets some inkling of how John Clare immersed himself in the trees and the wildflowers and the fens and the mists of winter and the burning sun of summer. He rushes down the hill, he has so much to write, has such a clear idea of what it is Clare would say, how the man's story should be told.

But exhaustion sets in. He's back at the cottage, his head bursting with ideas, his body exhausted and weak.

He types a few sentences but he can't write the rawness of what he experienced in the mist and trees and he falls asleep where he sits.

'Why do you talk about John Clare all the time?'

'Do I?'

'You're always reading about him and writing about him.'

'No, I'm not.'

'Yes you are.'

'That's bullshit.'

'You said you'd take us bowling on Saturday night and we ended up watching that crappy film on TV while you were writing.'

'I told you, the alley was booked out.'

'Because you didn't ring in time, because you were writing.'

'Well, why didn't you remind me, smart ass.'

'You told us not to disturb you.'

'You're just whinging.'

'Well, can we go bowling this weekend?'

'Not if you're going to whinge about it.'

He knows that writing about John Clare keeps him animated and determined. He gives himself, more and more, to the poet and his world. He tries to feel what Clare felt and he uses his own irrationality to divine the poet's. He persuades himself that the melancholy in him is a temporary, empathetic thing. But he knows that when Clare is gone, when the novel is finished, he'll have to face life. And life isn't something out there waiting for him. Life is what he has to get on with. Life is what he's supposed to be living or, at least, making an effort to live, *for the sake of the children.*

The phone rings. It's his wife.

'I think we need to talk,' she says.

And so they do.

He sits at the kitchen table that used to be theirs. He looks out on the trees he planted for the children's births.

'I don't want to tell you what to do but you really need to try to organise a few things for the kids. You know, bring them to things.'

'I was going to take them to the pictures but you'd brought them. I wish you'd let me know what you're doing, then I could plan accordingly.'

'It's not all about planning. Just doing things. On the spur of the moment.'

'Not always possible,' he says. 'There are other things – work, the book, life.'

Whatever that means!

'The kids are part of life.'

'Thanks for reminding me.'

'I'm not trying to fight with you. It's just that they seem a bit bored when they're out there.'

'Well that's because they don't want to get off their arses and do things, get out, go places, see things, explore.'

'But you have to do things they want to do, too.'

Christmas is a fortnight away and the towns and villages are awash with coloured rain. John's Christmas tree sits like a badly parked juggernaut on the kitchen floor. There's no escape from Christmas carols on the radio. It's a time for smiling, happy people.

At work, the round of parties has begun.

'I suppose we'll see you down the pub?'

'Of course!'

'Yeah, that'll be the day.'

His non-appearance is nothing new. None of the

usual, seasonal invitations arrive for drinks or dinner at friends' houses. This, too, he supposes, is part of being the bastard who walked out on his family.

He's in the local supermarket, at the back of a queue. He has the essentials for the week – milk, butter, vegetables, a small bag of potatoes.

At the checkout, the cashier smiles at him.

'Just picking up a few things,' he says.

'Not doing the Christmas shop yet?'

'No, I'll leave it a while. Get you some night when things are quiet.'

She laughs.

'You'll be hard pushed to find a night that's quiet from here to Christmas.'

'I must remember that.'

He pays and carries his one bag of groceries to the car.

All his life, he's known men in this position and now he's one of them. He has become one of those men who appeared in Savages or McEvoy's shops when he was a boy, bought their single box of groceries, tied it to the carrier of a bicycle and disappeared into the countryside.

eight

They're always there, Christmas, Easter, summertime, Halloween. Their cigarette butts dangle from the corners of their mouths, ash sprouting from well-sucked *Woodbine* and *Sweet Afton*. They wear their caps pulled down over eyes that are always in shadow. They're constantly at Cope's Corner. Early in the morning, late at night, always there in the pooled light from the street lamp, in the scant shelter from the rain, backs against the shop wall that fractures the wind.

I'm eight years old and these are grey, unshaven men, their clothes tattered and their teeth brown. These are men who can spit words without taking the Woodbine from between blue lips.

They're hard, bitter men who seldom smile but often smirk, men to be avoided on my way for messages or racing to catch the evening post. Sometimes, they jeer me across the open Square and, for those seconds, I'm a pig turning on a spit. I hear the taunts about my father's politics.

When they catch three or four of us together, they mouth things about sisters and mothers, things we don't understand but which bruise us.

'How's your sister, hah?'

'How's your mother?'

I both dread and hate the *corner boys*. It seems their only purpose is to torture the children and young women who can't avoid crossing the Square. Nothing moves that their eyes don't follow. They're a permanent judge and jury, a choir of cursing little Gods.

The corner boys exist in a world I believe I will never understand. Even the words, corner boys, are frightening. These boys are grown men who can cut and chill with a mouthful of mumbled curses. They have an air of viciousness. *Louts*, some people call them. *Sots*, other people say. They drink in relays, always, leaving two or three of their number at the corner to catch the passer-by. And, if their words can hurt, their fists can do more. These are the same men who get into fights behind the marquee when the local carnival is in full swing. I've seen them in the coloured lights, stepping from the shadows, their coats thrown across their arms, blood dripping from broken noses onto white shirts, eyes closing or closed from the battering they've taken, fists raw from the battering they've given.

These are the men who terrorise me on winter evenings and summer afternoons. I run the malice of their tongues while crossing the road to Cope's. Their voices echo like gunshots between McEvoy's and Abbot's, up past the Shamrock Bar, ricocheting back between Thompson's and Gannon's to McDonald's and Rice's. They fear no one and respect no one, their mouths always angled in sneers. Their clothes smell of drink and cigarettes and dampness but the weather never keeps them off the Square and they're never too drunk to laugh and their cigarettes are never smoked and never new.

Their place on the path, at the gable of the shop, is petalled with the short stumps of cigarettes and cobbled with the thick spits that drop like clots from dark mouths.

nine

This was not how John imagined life. He is lonely and battered by the good grace of Christmas. He is terrified and lost, without the slightest idea of where his life is going. He wants to finish his book because he believes there may be life for him after John Clare's life. But he's frightened by the thought of letting the poet go, of searching for something new to write, of not having something to do when the children are asleep and he can't sleep at all.

Sometimes, when the children are staying with him, he reads for them, well past their bedtime.

'I thought you were going to be writing tonight.'

'I will. I'll just finish this chapter.'

They're reading Roald Dahl.

'I can finish it, I'll read it out loud,' his daughter says

'It's all right. I want to see what happens.'

Anything to postpone the evil moment.

ten

At the end of the road, near the grass triangle where we gather in the evening, there's a mat of burnt, sodden fur. A man comes from one of the houses, carrying a sack and a shovel. He lifts the fur and we see legs dangling over the side of the shovel, what might be a head lolls. He holds the sack open and slides the burned animal inside. He scrapes the footpath where the animal lay down to die.

'Someone set fire to a dog,' Joe Whelan says. 'Some of the boys from the town. They tied a tin can to his tail and set him on fire at Carlow Gate and ran him down here.'

'Did you see it?'

'No. Mr Byrne told me. He threw water over it but it was nearly dead by then.'

We watch the man carry the sack across his garden and lay it gently on the grass. He starts to dig a hole.

'Whose dog was it?'

'Don't know. A stray, I think.'

Darkness is falling, and as we walk back up the terrace, the sound of digging follows us.

eleven

Christmas week has come the way a Christmas week should, days hard and bright and evening frost falling early. The skies are clear and the stars are fires in the dark beyond. John discovers, to his delight, that when the frost is this severe, he can hear the trains across the fields from Maganey. He has lived with the sound of trains for fifteen years, and there was before that the constant presence of trains in his life. His father, two of his uncles and both his grandfathers worked on the railways. In his student days, he worked his holidays on the permanent way. Trains are in his blood.

He sits with the children in the back garden, well wrapped against the cold, watching the stars through binoculars. They make up names for the constellations.

'That's the Great Bicycle, you can only see the front wheel of it from here. They see the saddle and the back wheel in Australia.'

'And that's the Noodle Pump.' His son laughs uproariously at his own joke.

They read Laurie Lee by torchlight, following his Christmas carollers through the valleys. Later, they sluice water down the road and, when it freezes, push each other along it on plastic sacks, tobogganing crazily. Their laughter echoes up the hill and across the white fields. When car lights appear, they scatter to the safety of the ditches.

The Christmas spirit has soaked John's heart, in spite of everything.

He lies awake, talking with the children about Santa and what he might bring and what he brought when John was young.

'What's the best thing about Christmas?'

His daughter thinks for a moment.

'Going to bed on Christmas Eve, leaving out the food for Santa, that's my favourite bit.'

'I prefer waking up,' his son says. 'Going down to the sitting room.'

'No, I prefer going to bed, you're never sure what he'll bring. I like the waiting. What's the best present you ever got, dad?'

'The best thing I ever got? My teddy bear. I was six. It was our first Christmas in the new house.'

He's working on a script for a radio programme about childhood Christmases and he gives a lot of thought to the corner boys. He wants them to be a part of the programme. As a child they had no redeeming mercies. But now he's forty years old, older than many of those men were when he was a boy, and he has begun to recognise some of the losses they suffered early in life, the isolation and pain. And, if Cope's Corner was their haunt, who is he to say it shouldn't have been? He has his own corners now, places he hangs around. Corners in his head where he slouches with his back to depression, angry eyes beading for a moving target. And, when a story comes back with a polite rejection slip, he has some small glimpse of how it must have felt to have no work in a time when work was the yardstick by which people's worth was measured. But work, for the corner boys, was limited to a half-day here and a few weeks there, snagging turnips or weeding beet. Disposable, hired and fired without consideration, they were the supply that outstripped demand.

They were men who lived alone down deserted roads, in cottages where the floors were bare and the *Irish Press* and *The News of the World* piled up in corners. They were men who sat, on the few occasions they went home, at ranges that panted the smoke of black, damp turf back into their clothes and hair.

Only on Christmas Day was Cope's Corner deserted. On that day alone the corner boys dispersed for dinner to the houses of married sisters. Christmas Day was their loneliest day, a yearly reminder of the absences in their lives.

They arrived uncertainly at the sisters' houses, unsettled by the niceties that awaited them, all their bravado falling away as they left the place where they were kings in companionship and headed off in separate directions. These were the men who sat, politely, through dinner and then left again in the early afternoon with excuses about the twilight coming down and forgotten bicycle lamps and card games they'd promised to attend. But the truth was that they couldn't stay because they lived in fear of being overtaken by a deep, creeping loneliness. They carried their Christmas spirit with them in naggins of whiskey or half dozens of stout, down the black laneways. And they were overtaken, by isolation and emptiness, on the long road home or in the cold, empty kitchens where even the radio was slow to play. Bent over the dead range they saw life for what it was, a heap of cold ash, frailer even than the corpse.

Now, there are no corner boys at Cope's, only a woman sheltering from the rain. The traffic thunders, the Square is rarely silent but the corner boys are gone.

When exactly was it that they left? Sometime while he was away at school, sometime in the late Sixties. One by one they melted from the street. Finally, the loneliness was just too much to take and a new-year promised nothing. One of them who found the courage to go went home and dragged a small brown case from beneath his bed and packed everything he owned and still had room to spare. In the morning, he pulled the door closed after him, put the key under a stone in the yard and caught the Dublin bus at Farrelly's, where he knew his comrades wouldn't see him. And, as the bus stopped on the Square, he sat on the side farthest from their gaze and kept his face to the window and then he was gone and no one knew, not his sister or his neighbours or the other corner boys. He was a fortnight in Birmingham before he wrote a short four lines to his sister with an address and a ten-shilling note for her children. And, once he'd left, a spell was broken and one by one, the others followed and only those who couldn't leave remained until they died.

And what was Birmingham, a new life or another procession of forlorn rooms above busy streets? The lonely Christmases at home were left for lonelier Christmases abroad. The corner boys trudged back from dead-end jobs, through fag-end bars, to tiny bed-sits in cities where they knew no one. Did they dream of poaching fish on the Lerr? Did they miss the clink of coins pitched and tossed on Keenan's Lane? And when they shuffled up some stairs were they thinking of a young girl they watched and loved one time, a long time ago? Did their memories gradually glimmer with a softer glow? Did home seem like a better place, a place where they could be boys again? Were these the dreams they spilled between the legs of the women who took pity on them? Or the nightmares that could never be drowned in drink?

John recognises that feeling. Acknowledges the part of them in him, the part of him in them. They had the power then to frighten him but no more power than he has now to frighten himself. He knows something of the dark roads and the empty house and the rage that has no target and rebounds, slapping his face like guilt. He catches glimpses of what was, what might have been and is envious of the man he sees. Often, the only feelings he discerns are loss and longing. He recognises the corner boys' escape for what it was and he recognises his own in it. They pretended and he does the same.

He works hard on that radio script, writing it for himself and, in some belated way, for the corner boys. They suspected, deep down, that there was no escape from the loneliness they carried inside and he suspects they were right. They were afraid of going, yet they left, only to discover a fear of returning. They dreamed of the past, yet the past smothered them. They lived in the shadow of a place they called home, the corner, the village they loved and despised in equal measure, and knew they'd never, ever go back to again. Not even for funerals. Not even their own.

He goes into the studio and records the programme for Christmas Eve, oblivious to the microphones and head-phones and tape turning slowly on the reel. This one's for them. Driving home, he listens to a cassette of the recording, and something of the season's blessing flows through him.

twelve

It's the morning of Christmas Eve. I'm nine years old. I open my eyes and lie in bed a moment. It's bright. A strange light is coming through the bedroom window but it's not the light of Christmas morning. It doesn't have the particular shimmer and glow that Christmas brings, the light that's brighter than the brightest summer day. I listen to the sounds from downstairs and then, as though she senses I'm awake, my mother calls from the kitchen and I stumble out of bed, into the busiest day of the year.

While I'm dressing, I try to remember just how many times I was sent down the village on messages the previous Christmas Eve. I settle on ten as a conservative estimate and I know that I stand a good chance of beating that figure this year.

In the kitchen, the reaction to my appearance is immediate.

'When you've had your breakfast, clean out the fire, bring in the sticks and coal, set the fire and light it and then I'll have a few things for you to do.'

My mother says this over her shoulder, without looking up from the mince pies she's making. My sister is in the back kitchen, and the BBC Light programme is playing on the radio.

I want to dream of a Christmas Eve when there's no work to be done, when we can enjoy the day but I know that will never happen. Instead, I hurry my breakfast, clean the fire, riddle the cinders, chop the sticks, fill the coal bucket, set and light the fire by which time the list is ready.

The ham from Copes, cream from Savage's, biscuits from McEvoy's, the paper from Abbots and stamps from Carrie Murphy in the Post Office.

'Is there anything else?' I enquire, as if there's even the vaguest hope of getting all the shopping done in one fell swoop!

'I'm sure there is,' my mother says, still not looking up from the mince pies. 'I'll think of it while you're doing that lot.'

I get the shopping bag from under the stairs and collect the money and the list from the table.

'Oh and, ah, four bottles of milk,' my mother adds.

I hate the clatter of milk bottles in the empty bag. It cramps my style, slows me down. Who ever saw a cowboy riding the prairie with milk bottles in his saddlebag? But I collect the empties and escape before she can come up with anything else.

Outside, the day is grey, cold and grey, but dry.

It only takes a second to saddle my horse, and I ride out through the gate, across the range that is Abbeylands, through the Rio Grande of Carlow Gate and on to the wide open plains of the Square. The Square where the corner boys are already in place. It's cold out here but that's the cowboy's life, riding fast and living free, and for those minutes I forget the clattering milk bottles in the shopping bag.

It's getting on for night-time. Darkness stains the bright air. The sky has cleared and the evening star is blinking over Rice's Hill. The Christmas tree is up, the turkey has arrived and I'm on my way down the village again but this time it's not so bad, just a handful of last-minute Christmas cards that won't get to their destinations on time but at least they'll be postmarked before the day.

It's always the same. Three or four cards arrive from people we'd forgotten, despite the meticulous list that my mother makes each January and puts in the decoration box in the attic, along with the crib and the lights that never work the following Christmas. Funny how the same things happen year after year, late cards, missing bulbs, the turkey arriving uncleaned, chips off the plasterwork crib figures.

At Flaherty's, I meet Olive Hunt from next door, labouring home with a shopping bag of groceries. We smile. Olive is OK. She's a girl but she's sound.

'I hope I don't have to do any more messages,' she says.

'Take your time,' I advise her, 'then the shops'll be closed.'

She slackens her pace.

'If you want to hang on, I'll be back up with you. I just have to post these.'

She drops the shopping bag and sits on the low wall. I race on, up to the Post Office, past the corner boys still on duty. Opening the Post Office door, I plunge into the chaos of stamp licking and furious last-minute card writing.

'Four stamps please, Carrie.'

I stamp and post and run.

Olive is still sitting on Flaherty's wall, chewing half a Trigger bar. She's kept the other half for me. I take one handle of the shopping bag and we trudge up the hill past Paddy Byrne's.

Our talk turns to Santa and what we hope he'll bring and what we asked for and what we'll probably get – not always the same things!

We part at the gate and I meet my mother at the front door.

'Just in time,' she says, handing me a box of matches.

Dina Whelan is ringing the Angelus from the church-yard and, as ever, we light the Christmas candle in the window while the bell is tolling. I feel the spell of Christmas descending around me.

Night falls. The radio tells me that Santa has left the North Pole but my mother assures me that he won't be here until the early hours of the morning. Even so, walking down the garden to collect sprouts, a flashlight in one hand and a saucepan in the other, I warily scan the sky.

This is my first year to be allowed to midnight Mass. That in itself is a sign that I'm growing up. But I don't want to find myself face to face with a reindeer when I get back home.

'Don't worry, you'll be well asleep,' my mother says.

My father arrives home from work. He's waited for the seven o'clock train, bringing my brother from holiday sorting work in the Post Office in Dublin. And bringing, too, the yellow cake, the legendary concoction that comes each year from my Uncle Andy's grocery shop in Athy. It gets its name from the topping of almond icing, sweet, bright yellow and sticky. To my delight, no one else will eat it but me.

My mother interrupts with a call from the back-kitchen. 'I forgot to get you to drop Noel Byrne's present down to him. Run over with it now like a good boy.'

Noel is her Godchild, born on Christmas Eve. Is that a good thing or a bad thing? He and I have often discussed the question. On the one hand, it means extra presents at Christmas but it also means there's never a party because the day is always too busy. We never can decide.

I put on my coat and saddle up again, my fourteenth journey that day, only this time it's easier. No rush, mosey on down, riding slow across the dark empty prairie. I scan the sky for the lights of the sleigh but it's still too early. Like my mother said, I'll be well asleep.

In Byrne's I gulp a glass of lemonade, stuff four Kimberley biscuits into my mouth and head off again.

At home, the house smells of Christmas. Ham cooking. Mince pies. Boot polish as the shoes are shone for midnight Mass. In the sitting room there's a different smell. Pine needles from the Christmas tree. While the rest of the family are chatting and laughing in the kitchen, I sit in the shadowy sitting room, lit only by the tree and the flames from the open fire. I dream of the next day, of Santa's arrival.

And then my brother comes in, carrying a record player he's bought in Dublin. He sets it up in the corner of the room and then goes out again, down to McDonald's to borrow some records from Frank. Twenty minutes later he's back with an armful of LPs, among them Mario Lanza. We sit and listen to the voice from the speaker. After the others have gone out, I put the needle back to the start of the record and listen again. The fire glimmers, and pine needles stab the light from the coloured bulbs. All is well with the world. It's the loveliest night of the year.

There's something about that first midnight Mass, a heightening of the senses. As though I've never been in the church in Castledermot at night before. But, of course, I have, for October devotions, benediction, funerals, All Souls and All Saints nights. But tonight I'm wide-awake and everything is different. The shadows are sharper around the altar, the lights are brighter, there's an atmosphere in the church and it's full — or almost full. Not like the October devotions with the handful of elderly people squeezing up aganst the tepid radiators. And us kids lurking at the back of the men's gallery, in the shadows that allow just enough light for a game of twenty-five, but enough gloom to keep us hidden from the failing eyes of the Parish Priest.

Tonight is a night for warmth and light and promises fulfilled. And there's plenty of style — new hats and coats that have come, at least, from Carlow and, in a few cases, from Dublin. And there's one outfit that's travelled from London. It's modelled slowly all the way down the catwalk of the main aisle, right to the very front seat. The adults around me on the gallery lean forward to identify the face beneath the hat and, having done so, nod to each other, as if to say: *Of course, of course, sure we should have known.*

Behind us, the choir members are taking their places in the corner of the gallery. Mrs Aylmer plays a few notes on the organ. The altar boys come out in their black soutanes and white surplices. The candles are lit, the church fills up, the priest appears and the Mass begins.

Sometime after the gospel, my eyelids begin to sag. I drift in and out of the remainder of what's happening. The priest's voice goes on somewhere out there and then the choir is singing and the congregation twists and twines to the altar rails and back again. The closing blessing and the choir rises as one great voice. *Gloria in excelsis Deo* spills out along the air, the sound carrying after us as we walk across the yard outside the church. Voices mesh and accents that have changed in a year abroad recount well-told stories. I walk on with my parents. My brother and sister lag behind, meeting old friends from school, catching up on the goings-on in Kilburn, Birmingham and Boston.

On the Square, the corner boys are still in place, hands driven deep into their pockets. Last in to Mass, first out after Communion time.

Across the School Lane the streetlights are on, the only night of the year when the village streets remain lit through the darkness. And then we're home and I'm in bed and my father, tucking me in, reminds me the Sandman is coming. And Santa Claus!

From downstairs, I hear voices. My parents, my brother and sister, Reg and Adrian O'Connell from next door, someone else – a voice I can't identify. Who is it? Is it …? But my head fills with the music I heard earlier in the church, and I strain to catch the sound of sleigh bells. Did I hear them? The music comes back again. A voice, a choir, a carol fills my dreams.

thirteen

This first Christmas at the cottage is not nearly as awful as he'd expected. He leaves the tree, untrimmed, flaunting its red ribbons. The children say it looks ridiculous. He watches them make a dramatic production of negotiating their way around and under and through it while going to and from the fridge.

'You should really call this place The Tree House.'

He tells them he likes its simplicity.

They look at him as though he's the simple one and they laugh until tears run down their cheeks.

He's making a Christmas cake and the children are barred from the kitchen. He's using a recipe given to him by Ruth, a friend at work. It's her mother-in-law's and it comes with the promise of never having failed!

He creams the butter and sugar. His hands are greasy and the mixture clings to his fingers. He breaks six eggs and adds these and the flour alternately, beating the thickening mix as he goes. His wrist is sore and his elbow stiff but the cake is coming together, blending and changing colour. He opens the packets of mixed peel and cherries and sultanas and raisins and nuts and sprinkles and mixes and folds. He greases the cake-tin and lines it with brown paper and begins to pour the mixture. It's not pouring as he'd hoped. Just then the kitchen door opens a fraction and he glances up to see four eyes peering through the crack.

'What is it?' he asks sharply.

'Are you finished?'

'Not yet.'

'Can we lick the bowl?'

He looks back. The cake mix has begun to slide over the side of the tin.

'Look, why don't you just keep out of my way for a while, don't annoy me now. I asked you keep out of my way, just do that.'

The door closes again.

He remembers his own determination to be the one to lick the spoon and the bowl after his mother had made the cakes, to taste that soft, sweet blend.

Opening the oven door, he slides the tin inside and then closes it quickly. But nothing of the smell or taste of Christmas lingers after his cake-making. He looks at the kitchen table, littered with bowls and butter wrappers and eggshells and flour and suddenly, senselessly feels cheated and angry.

Calling the children from the sitting room, he gestures towards the bowl and spoon on the table. While he washes the rest of the dishes, the inevitable happens.

'You said I could be first.'

'I did not.'

'You did, you said I could have the spoon first.'

'Well, I'm hardly going to lick the spoon after your dirty, smelly tongue was all over it.'

'But I'm supposed to lick it after you!'

'Yeah, 'cause you're a pig, you won't know the difference.'

He listens from the scullery as the bowl is tugged between them.

'Give it to me.'

'No.'

'Bitch.'

'Shut up, you little whinger.'

He hears the plastic bowl clatter across the table and he's in the kitchen, whipping bowl and spoon from their hands, ushering them through the hallway.

'Bed,' he says.

'But it's only half seven ….'

'She started it.'

'Bed, now. No more fighting, none of it. Bed, now. Go.'

'We haven't had our tea.'

'Tough. You should have thought of that.'

'It's not fair, it's ….'

'No more,' his voice booms in the hallway and they fall silent. 'Four minutes, wash teeth, get changed, then bed.'

Three hours later and the children have been to bed and up again for a late supper and are now asleep. The unwashed mixing bowl is soaking in the kitchen sink. The house is filled with the Christmas smell of the slowly cooking cake but the place feels empty, cold and empty.

He brings the children to visit his father. They exchange presents and Jack, as always, fishes two bars of chocolate from the bottom drawer of the kitchen press and gives them to the children.

He takes them to visit his mother's grave and they put a holly wreath on it.

His son finds an old plastic wreath in the cemetery dump. It says *Nana* in faded white and pink plastic roses.

'I think Nana would like this.'

John shakes his head, thinking his mother-in-law would, most definitely, not be impressed.

'I think she would,' his daughter titters.

'I'm not sure,' he says. 'It's a bit faded.'

'She can wash it. She'll like it,' the boy maintains.

'All right, if you want. But you give it to her, not me.'

Nana is anything but impressed but she bites her tongue. He suspects she thinks he put his son up to it!

He wants this to be a normal Christmas. Neither his wife nor he wants the children to have two Christmases. They don't want to be sucked into some kind of competition. Some things are sacred and Christmas is one of them.

On Christmas Eve he moves back to be there when Santa arrives, as he will, as he always does.

Waking in the house that was *home* is a strange experience. It feels unnatural but, at the same time, it feels right and the rightness has to do with the needs of the children, not with his emotions. He lies for a moment, remembering their first Christmas here, as a newly married couple. The bare floors, the empty rooms, the decorations in the kitchen and sitting room, the flags that doubled as curtains on the windows, the fire burning in the grate. This was *home, our house, our home, our dream*. And they were happy. Will they ever, he wonders, be happy again?

Christmas Day is the same day it has been since his daughter's birth. There are no arguments, no lost tempers. The overseas phone-calls come and are made. The day passes in an unspoken but seasonal good will. The children play with their toys. They watch *Willy Wonka and the Chocolate Factory*. They play cards into the early hours and he stays a second night.

St. Stephen's Day takes up where Christmas Day had finished. There's the traditional dinner in his parents-in-law's house and then a long walk, TV films and another late round of cards. It's after midnight when they get back to the house and he helps put the children to bed.

Just before driving back to the cottage, he goes in to kiss them goodnight. They both appear to be asleep. As he's pulling the bedclothes around his daughter she whispers, without opening her eyes, without really waking: 'I'm glad you're back in the family.'

At the hall door, he hugs his wife. He makes it to the car before he cries.

The cottage is freezing but, otherwise, everything is as he left it. He lights a fire in the sitting room and makes some tea, cuts a slice of Christmas cake and sits by candlelight, listening to the Leonard Cohen CD the children gave him.

He's happy that some part of Christmas has been normal, whatever normal means. As far as he can tell, the children were happy in their days. He has promised that if snow falls he'll come and collect them and they'll go tobogganing on Mullaghcreelan Hill.

He thinks about his wife. He can't settle on any one big reason why they've gone their separate ways. No single day when love ended and the rest of their lives began. He can't remember a day when he imagined everything had changed from the day before. There is no one argument, no row that was left unresolved, not even a disagreement to which he could point and say: *That's the reason why.*

Sitting long into the morning, he reaches the conclusion that nothing can happen, nothing will change, their lives will still be hanging like frozen clothes on a washing line, until such time as one or the other says something. But he knows, too, that what seems clear and easy in that peculiarly profound time between midnight and dawn will prove less clear and easy in the full light of day.

This week, he thinks, this week we'll talk about it.

In the yellow light, he allows himself the company of other Christmases.

One in the late Sixties, sleeping in the sitting room, listening to Paul Simon singing *The Dangling Conversation.*

One in the early Seventies, a dance in the youth club. His first kiss in the shadow of the sycamore outside its door. That was on a night between Christmas and New Year, a girl whose eager tongue met his. A week later, they were dancing together, again, and he could feel the shape of her body pressed against his and could smell an autumnal scent of apples from her hair. And she was wearing a lime green dress and her eyes were the brightest he had ever seen. And he was in love with her. And he couldn't believe it when, in the last frantic dance of the dying night, she whispered, 'I love you'.

And The Poppy Family was singing '*Which way you going Billy?*'

He still knows all the words.

And there were other Christmases and other loves and presents and cards. Vincent Van Gogh's letters that set him off in search of the man. A love letter inside a Christmas card. The card went up on the mantelpiece, for his parents' benefit, but the letter stayed in his pocket to be read and re-read while he walked the dogs across the wintry fields. All those Christmases and all that happiness and so much love, disco lights, the darkness outside, the dreams and sleep.

And then he turns off the music, goes and stands on the backdoor step and looks across the valley. The occasional light burns but, for the most part, people are sleeping. Christmas is over.

fourteen

What went on at the back of the church? Sometime around the year of my birth the Blessed Virgin appeared in a rocky grotto, to a kneeling French girl called Bernadette Soubirous. I could never fathom what a French girl was doing kneeling on the bank of a tiny stream in Castledermot. But it had happened. The Blessed Virgin came and spoke to her and so important was the moment that they were frozen and there they remained, in everlasting apparition.

It's a spring afternoon and we've come to see them, crossing the narrow brook that separates our prayers from the rest of the village. We watch for a blink, a sneeze, a sign of life in the statues. We tickle the feet of the Blessed Virgin. She ignores us. Her eyes stay fixed on heaven. We twirl daisies under Bernadette's concrete nostrils. Finally, in exasperation, I whisper *fuck* in her ear and run away in terror at what I've done, expecting the wrath of God to strike me dead before I reach the street.

And other things go on at the back of the church. In winter, at night, as we altar boys close the church door after evening benediction, the smell of incense on our skin, we see the occasional ghosts of the living disappear behind the grotto. Down there, in the shelter of the convent wall, where the grass is long and the darkness untroubled, these apparitions melt into the shadows.

We hang around the gable end. Sometimes, we hear them giggle, sometimes we hear them sigh but, mostly, we hear nothing at all.

'They're riding,' one of the altar boys says. He's thirteen, a couple of years older than the rest of us. 'I betcha they're riding. My brother says there's always riding going on down there.'

We nod sagely. We have some vague idea of what he means but not much.

'I'll give you half a Trigger if you go down and look and see who it is.'

'I will in my bollicks. Do you think I'm a complete sack?'

'Yeah!'

It's an afternoon in summer, Olive Hunt and Marion Kelly and myself have brought our jam-jars and we're fishing in the shadow of the grotto, luring pinkeens from beneath the rocks. From time to time, we glance up at the frozen figures behind us.

'I'm nearly sure I saw her moving.'

Suddenly, we're nervous. There's not a birdsong to be heard, nothing but the summer stillness.

'She moved, she moved.'

We scatter, terrified, jam jars forgotten, racing through the long grass in Keatley's field, afraid to look behind, waiting for the hand of God's mother to fall on our shoulders. Someone is screaming. I'm screaming. We're all screaming and the heat of the day tries to trip us but we keep running, the dry grass and thistles whipping our bare feet, running till we're out on the safety of the road.

On July nights, teenagers gather on the wall behind the grotto and there are always two who stay when the rest have gone, risking the wrath of the Parish Priest in the warm twilight.

fifteen

Each year there are these days between Christmas and New Year, when he analyses and resolves. The last days of 1992 are like that.

The year just ending has been the most painful and destructive in his family's life. Sometimes he wakes and wonders if they will survive. Sometimes he thinks he's dreaming. But always he tries to find a place where the pain might be lessened and the loneliness diluted.

He thinks a lot about his own childhood, his brother and sister away at school and college, leaving him – effectively – an only child. That afforded him a great deal of freedom but it also anchored him at the centre of an often volatile relationship between his parents.

There were many times he'd wished they'd go their separate ways and let him live in peace. It wasn't that life was constantly unhappy but that a perpetual, shadowy uncertainty dawdled at the edge of every day.

As a small boy, what he yearned for, more than anything, was stability. Instead, he got good times shattered by burning quarrels that flamed out of nowhere.

His first responsibility in life, it seemed, was to act as a conciliator between his parents. He longed for Christmases or those short weeks in late September when his brother, Jarlath, was home. His presence lifted the burden of responsibility from John's shoulders. His brother didn't seem to take things as seriously as he did. And he sorted things out. As long as he was there John didn't worry. But when his brother was away, he was back at the core of a volcano that was as random as it was intense.

The battles he witnessed were sometimes no more than two stubborn people refusing to concede to each other. But sometimes they ran deeper and the silences went on for days, quiet harbingers of troubles still to come. In the worst of those silences he'd act as go-between for his parents.

All he knew was that he was uncertain in the good times and bitterly unhappy when the shouting matches exploded in the night and left him shivering on the stairs, afraid to intervene and afraid to go back to bed. Counting to a hundred, listening to the endless, pointless round-about of argument that never progressed, only echoed like the next hundred and the next.

He grew up, caught in the crossfire, and it continued in his absence at school and college and was there to welcome him home when he returned to live and teach in the village. Finally, it died with his mother, just as it would have done with his father.

He could never fathom, and still can't, what exactly it was that brought the schoolteacher from the West of Ireland and the railwayman from the Midlands together. Politics was hardly enough to cement such a relationship.

For the child caught in this maelstrom, it was a night-mare, a constant ache in the pit of his stomach, a cruelty that is hard to forgive.

'It's cold in here,' his son says

They've just arrived back from Athy. The fire has gone out in the sitting room.

'Bring in some sticks from the kitchen and I'll get it going.'

'I brought in the groceries from the car. You do it.'

The boy points to his sister.

'You are such a lazy asshole,' she says.

'I'm not doing everything. You do nothing.'

'Who brought in the coal in mam's?'

He wants to go somewhere he can't hear them but the voices follow him into the kitchen.

'Why don't you have central heating anyway?'

'Because this is not my house and we won't be here for ever.'

'Says who?'

'Says I! Now light the fucking fire yourselves.'

He storms out of the cottage, gets into the car and drives a couple of miles through the darkness.

Everything is confusion. He's catching the children in the trap his parents laid for him.

Trouble springs from nowhere. Another night they're sitting in the kitchen, finishing dinner. Suddenly, his daughter is crying.

'What is it?'

'Nothing.'

'It must be something. Go and check the fire inside,' he tells his son.

To his surprise, the boy goes without a word.

'Now, tell me. What's the problem?'

'Nothing, I said, just nothing.'

'It'd be good if you talked to me.'

'Would it? It won't solve anything.'

'Not if I don't know what the problem is.'

'If I have to tell you it's obviously not important to you.'

The door opens.

'Just hang on inside.'

The door closes again.

'Now, tell me … please.'

'We're always fighting. Every time we're here someone is fighting. I thought it was going to be great out here but it isn't, is it?'

'It was good in the summer.'

'But it's not summer now. It can't be summer all the time. Are we supposed to wait for summer?'

He shakes his head.

John and his wife are sitting in the car outside their house, her house. They're discussing the feasibility of telling the children the whole truth but they decide the time isn't right. To tell them will be to face that fact and articulate it, fully, themselves and that means one or the other of them nailing a final black flag to the mast. It comes down to accepting that everything positive between them as a couple counts, in the end, for nothing. None of the times they've been through, none of the kindness they've bestowed or received is enough to keep them together. The sense of failure is agonising.

He resolves, each time the children leave, that the next time there'll be no arguments, no shouting and screaming, no tears. He lives his life after the facts. And each time he fails.

It's a Saturday afternoon, early January, and he's spring-cleaning the cottage. He finds a cup under the children's bed. It's been there for a couple of days and there's a ring of congealed orange juice around the rim. He doesn't know exactly what it is about the sight of that cup but it takes his breath away. He sits on the bed and cries for a long time. There's something so sad, so childish, and so desolate about it. It resurrects memories of his own child-hood nights and raps his knuckles, reminding him that he has no answers.

An invitation comes, to read at a Spring Festival in a Cathedral. He isn't sure if he should. He walks up through the woods, thinking about it, trying to make his mind up.

On Sunday afternoons and through the summer time, Mullaghcreelan Hill teems with families, milling around the picnic tables, children screaming between the trees. But on wet Sunday mornings the place is deserted. The bluebells and, later, the foxgloves grow in places where the children never run. The furze-bushes are a brighter yellow in the rain. On the other side of the hill, away from the picnic tables, the trees thin out and give way to rolling, ochre fields

This is a place with its own gospel of colour and change. There's an austerity out here on the hill but a freedom, too. No peeling walls and high ceilings and no question of whatever passes for God having to squeeze under doors or through gaps in the window frames. All he has ever found out here is a promise but that's as much as he has ever hoped for.

So, he walks up there, again, and thinks about the invi-tation and decides he'll accept and use the opportunity to write and read something new.

He works on a piece about birth and death, hoping to bring his lost brothers and sisters inside the door of a church at last.

sixteen

My mother has gone on like that, hawing like that, each breath grating and scraping along her throat, emerging into the air like an ache. Each time we open the door of her hospital room we're met by the sound of her shallow, painful breathing. That breathing becomes a process that clings to life and, at the same time fights against the notion of survival. And, each time we leave the room, the rasping notes follow, then wither as the door is closed.

The hospital corridor, with its gestures towards life, is a relief after the endless uneasiness of the sighing and gasping. Death beckons my mother, like a friend, but still she won't and can't go.

I'm surprised by this unwillingness to break free. My mother has spent her life believing in the will and mercy of God and now, given the chance of substantiation, she seems to have balked at the gateway. Instead of rushing to the arms of the Saviour, she lies stubborn and distressed in an unfamiliar hospital bed.

Day and night and day again. All this second week the breathing goes on. It seems nothing to do with life and everything to do with torment and anguish.

A week ago she'd been rambling, talking about the other children. But there were only three of us and we were there by her bedside. She'd gone on about how we were to take care of the other children, to look after them, not to let them get cold.

Keep them well wrapped up, she'd whispered. *Make sure they're well wrapped up before you take them outside.*

My father had leaned across her bed and patted her hand and told her *yes, yes*, he'd make sure they were well wrapped up and, *yes*, he'd check before he took them outside and, *yes*, he'd be careful with them.

And, then, her voice again, with a hardness I couldn't fathom.

You weren't before.

I sensed a deep and real pain in him and that was bewildering.

My father had never been a man to show torment but it was there in his eyes, there in the way he winced.

Sitting, now, with my parents is like sitting with two strangers, not the people I grew up with, the people whose moods I watched like signs of weather. Their marriage had been fiery most of the time, but I've never seen this deep, bleak, raw anguish before. I've never heard that terrible desolation in my mother's voice, never seen that look of absolute confusion on my father's face.

But his reaction surprised me even more. There was no flash of anger, no rush to have the last word. Instead, he agreed with her, patted her hand and ran his long fingers through her thin hair and massaged her temples, as though he could bring back the quickness that had gone from her brain.

Each day in the past week my mother has gone over and over the questions about the other children. Sometimes, when I'd been there alone with her, she'd ask me to check that they were well wrapped up and I played my father's part and reassured her and touched her hand and massaged her forehead with 4711 Cologne. And she'd stop her rambling talk.

And then the breathing started, sharp and shallow.

It doesn't necessarily mean anything, the nurses said. *It might be the start of something or just a temporary blip, it really is too early to tell.*

That's what they said but we knew otherwise. We recognised the code of kindness.

That was the second full week since my mother's stroke and life went on, had to go on. Work and all the rest of it continued, so we took it in turns to sit with her.

It reminded me of the factory shift-work I'd done in a card factory one summer. It was something odd, something undemanding and dull. Morning. Afternoon. Evening. Night.

My father has retired from work by now but he can't stay at the hospital all the time. There are things to be done at home and this situation, the doctors say, could go on for weeks or months. We have to learn to pace ourselves, they say.

So we take it in turns to be at the hospital. It's still early enough in my mother's illness for us to feel that someone should be there all the time.

In case, we say, just in case …

We never finish the sentence.

In case she makes a miraculous recovery, starts to talk sense again, is able to move? Hardly.

In case she dies?

That's it. But no one says as much, none of us comes out and says we fear her dying alone.

So, we take our turns at being here. Sleeping in the hard armchair. Chatting with the night-nurses when they bring us tea at twelve and five.

And it goes on, a third week and a fourth. We talk about taking her home.

Not yet, the doctors say. *Another week and we'll see.*

At home, people still call to the house to enquire about her. Once they see the car in the drive they come in search of news.

And we tell them what we can.

No change.

And they say, *that's good, she's stabilised, that's good.*

In school, pupils come to me after class to enquire about her, teenagers whom she taught as children in the village primary school.

The weeks take on a kind of insensibility. The drama of the first days is gone but the routine that has replaced it isn't authentic either. Spring is coming, mid-February, daffodils piking the cold ground, haws and whitethorns brandishing their buds, but it's hard to be enthusiastic about any of this.

That's when I first recognise the difference between the customary and the superficial. Life has changed, but it isn't just driving the hundred-mile round trip to and from Dublin, it isn't just the sudden waking in the middle of the night thinking the phone has rung. It's nothing as dramatic as that. Instead, it's the absence of purpose in ordinary things. Life has become a double negative but a negative just the same.

And, if I'm lost, I see the complete havoc in my

father's life. He's sixty-nine years old but he's hale and hearty. He enjoys life to the full. He loves his garden and politics and village life but none of these is enough. Suddenly, I see a dependence on my mother that I'd never imagined. I become aware of the depth of the love between them and not only through their inability to express it.

My mother can't communicate her feelings and my father has no one to whom he can convey his.

Tonight, I'm here in the hospital. Doing my stint, as I've done so many other nights over the past four weeks. Sitting, reading, hearing the hoarse breath and not hearing it. My mother's slim hold on her life has become a kind of background to my own. Now and then she snores, a loud, shuddering breath, before returning to the heavy, steady gasping which gestures towards life or, at least, existence.

In the early hours, the nurses come to turn my mother and I leave the room and walk the corridor.

At that hour the hospital is almost perfectly quiet. Only the undertone of the nurses' shoes on the soft vinyl reminds me that I'm not alone in the building.

Outside, a fresh white day is surfacing, spring, but without the heat that the early season sometimes brings.

I walk to the end of the corridor and stand at the glass wall that overlooks the car park. I count the scatter of cars angled in the white-lined emptiness, my own among them. Then I count the empty spaces. It's a ritual I've gone through for weeks. Count the cars and count the empty spaces. This morning the score is seventeen to sixty-three.

I know, even before they say. I know. I know by the way that the nurses are standing outside the door.

One of them smiles, shyly, and says, *She's gone.*

For an instant I have a reckless vision of my mother, all her girlhood energy recaptured, racing across the hospital lawns, away, gone, escaped back into childhood. I'm tempted to laugh out loud. But even as the thought crosses my mind I'm nodding.

Would you like to spend a few minutes with her?

I nod again.

The nurse opens the room door for me and I step inside. She waits a moment, watching, checking that I'm all right and then leaves me alone.

I walk to the window at the other end of the room and stand there, my back to my mother. I'm waiting for some noise, some movement. I can't believe that death brings such stillness. And then I turn and look at her. Her skin still holds the last stain of life. Her face has lost the pinched, strained expression that has haunted it for weeks. Now there's a softer, more familiar look to it and a serenity. I've heard people talk about the peace and repose of death. Now I'm seeing it.

She looks content, released but not into something new, released back into the easier, more enjoyable times of years before. Her face has that look I sometimes saw when she was standing at our front wall, late on a summer evening, the gardening done, talking to Mrs O'Connell or Mr and Mrs Hunt. It's a look that says: *I've got that out of the way and now I can enjoy the pleasure of a chat and the bit of gossip.*

It's a look I haven't seen in a long time and I'm happy for her.

And then I start talking to her in my head.

Do you remember the day my tricycle broke? Do you remember the way it lay in pieces at the back of the garage wall for months afterwards? I have no idea what age I was but I remember it clearly.

Do you remember my First Communion? There's a photograph somewhere, taken by the chemist, in the garden at the back of his house. White shorts, white shirt, sleeveless white pullover, yellow tie, white prayer book, white ankle socks, white sandals. It's all there in black and white, only the yellow tie and my suntanned face and hands and legs have faded. The way your colour will fade in the next few hours.

Do you remember the liquorice pipes you bought me every Saturday night in Smith's? Six, you said, one a day for the rest of the week. They were always gone by Sunday evening.

And the dozen ginger cakes from Bradbury's bakery. And the car tyres we had in the garden of the house in the Low Terrace, the tyres that were our horses —Orange Layer and Cho-Cho? And Joe Whelan and myself trying to rob gooseberries from under your nose?

But she doesn't remember. If she still has the capacity for memory, she's remembering another time and other children, the children at the bottom of the garden.

My parents met at a local dance. The few photographs there are of them, from the late Thirties and early Forties, show a handsome couple. My father was working then on the railway in Athy. My mother had come from Galway to teach in the National School.

After their marriage, a small, wartime affair, they settled in Castledermot.

People talk about all this in the days that follow her death. Callers to the house remember when *Miss Bray* first came to the village. Middle-aged men recall their first days in school. Others have stories of how she steered them through scholarship exams, sometimes against their will. People of my parents' age tell me where she lodged when first she came to Castledermot. I learn more about her early life than I've ever known. Her involvement in the local tennis club, how she'd been the only Catholic in the badminton club and had been *encouraged* by the Parish Priest, her school-manager, to leave it but had refused.

I wish people had been this forthcoming when she was alive. But in small communities, death opens doors of memory for a day or two and allows another part of the truth to slip through.

The schoolchildren line the main street of the village, from Behan's garage to the church, as the hearse carrying her body arrives. The church is packed.

This morning, as we take her from the church to the cemetery, hundreds of people file behind the hearse to Coltstown. We stand around the grave and hear the prayers and brace ourselves against the bitter wind that sweeps from Knockpatrick, across the valley and between the tombstones. We listen to the clay ringing on the coffin lid and then the softer sound of clay on clay until, finally, the last respects have all been paid and we're left alone with memory.

In the late afternoon, when everyone has gone, my sister, Dolores, takes our father back up to visit the grave, to take the name-cards from the wreaths piled high on the fresh clay.

But, even now, there's so much we don't know.

My mother was almost fifty years old when I was born so I never saw the younger, freer, and probably happier days of my parents' lives. By the time I was old enough to know, money was a constant problem. With my older brother in college and my sister in boarding school there was never enough for comfort. But education was the most important thing in life, worth any sacrifice.

I assume my parents came to the house on the Low Terrace, full of happiness and hope. It was a semi-detached house with three bedrooms, a kitchen and a toilet. No bathrooms then but it did have an enormous garden and my father set about making it productive.

It's all black and white at this distance, like the photographs of them seated outside the back door, my mother in the newly planted orchard, my father sitting in a chair in the yard, a dog at his feet.

There are later photographs, Jarlath as a baby on our aunt's knee, Dolores and her friends playing with dolls and, later still, the three of us on the huge swing at the back of the house, like steps of stairs.

I have my own images also.

My Aunt Bridie coming to mind me. She was the ideal aunt, unmarried, nursing in Tullamore, good-humoured, generous, a great one for a bawdy story.

My parents all dolled-up for a Labour Party dance. Tucking me in before they went. Promising two bars of Fry's cream in the morning. Waking to find the chocolate on the bedside table.

Summer evenings in the garden, picking lettuce and scallions for the tea. That garden that my father kept in order – a place for everything and everything in its place. Fruit bushes, apple trees and vegetables in beds and drills. And then the small wilderness near the hedge that separated our garden from the football-pitch, the wilderness where Joe Whelan and myself bellied our way through Indian wars.

But we didn't know.

People knew, of course they did. My parents knew, the midwife, the doctor, they knew. Neighbours who had been through the same thing themselves, they all knew. And the priests and the extended family knew.

But my parents knew most deeply. They had that experience, the expectation, the months of waiting and all the moody twists and turns along that road. The bad days in the pregnancy when it was as much as my mother could do to get to work. Putting in the hours in the old school, the constant morning sickness. Trying to keep the children interested. Struggling home again after school, the road getting longer week by week. The terrible tiredness and, in spite of that, the knowledge that it all must take its course. There were no short cuts. All she could do was see things through. Go to work, teach all day, come home and look after my brother and sister, cook and wash and bake and iron and wait.

And the measureless nights lying awake, trying to find some relief and comfort. Nights when she may have dared to dream, nights when she put names on the unborn, when she risked imagining the tone of each voice, no more than that. That was enough. On that she could begin to build a future that gave her unborn child good health, an education, a modicum of happiness, the makings of a life. She allowed herself those dreams, let the life spin out from her through the years. She dared the future. Maybe that was her mistake.

I can imagine her seeing it that way. Thinking that was where she went wrong in tempting God, giving a life before the life was finally given. She probably saw hope as a sin. Who could blame her?

Her generation had been taught not to hope. Daring to hear the voices of unborn children, to imagine their laughter, to listen to their games, to picture them, to call those unborn children in for their tea, to give them a place at the kitchen table was a conceit deserving of the wrath of God.

I remember her voice in the evening time. Joe Whelan and myself in Whelan's garden, smoking between the potato drills, sheltering a half Woodbine between us under the broad leaves of the Aran Banners. She stood on the back step, calling my father and myself for our tea. He buried the tines of his fork in the soil and lifted his coat from where it hung on the branch of an apple tree, his small formality.

But I waited, breathing deeply, expelling the taste of tobacco from my mouth and waving away the smoke whose smell might cling to my shirt. And she called my name a second time and then a third and I knew it was time to go.

And there were other evenings like that. Evenings when Joe and myself sat on the ditch between Whelan's and Behan's, watching Tom Forrestal's heavy horse as it pulled a plough up and down the long garden, drilling the soil. Evenings when I was so lost in watching the feathered feet lift so heavily and fall so carefully that I heard nothing until Mr Whelan's hand rested on my shoulder.

Your mother is calling you for your supper. I'd say you should be going in.

And he was right.

Life on the Low Terrace was safe. We knew everyone and everyone knew us. Twenty-two houses, semi-detached, single-storied. Stanley's; the Shop Paddy Byrne's; Tom Byrne's; Condron's; Whelan's; Howe's; Kinsella's; Behan's; Whelan's next-door; our house; Hickey's; Mrs Holligan; O'Rourke's; Kelly's; Thorpe's; O'Connell's; Core's; Lawler's; Corrigan's; Mrs Merrin's; the other Kelly's; the Cobbler Lawler's. That was our small, safe community where life went on in spite of everything. There were the little tragedies that were talked about and overcome, more or less. And the greater tragedies that we children never got to hear about.

My home was on the Low Terrace and I had other homes there.

Kinsella's, where Mammy K and Nan minded me. Later, the Kinsella girls moved to Birmingham but they kept the house and they still came back every summer and I still visited them.

O'Rourke's, where I got mashed potatoes and chopped cabbage and enormous mugs of milk for my dinner.

Whelan's, where I spent half my childhood playing with Joe.

Behan's, where John had a projector that amazed us by throwing pictures onto the wall from photographic negatives.

And Byrne's, where Noel, whose birthday fell on Christmas Eve, never had a party, but my mother always remembered because she was his godmother.

And beyond the end of the Terrace, beyond Carlow Gate and the ruins of the old town wall, there was another world. The gregarious streets of the village and the Square where the corner-boys hung around the gable end of Cope's shop, watching the world and providing a commentary on everything that happened and many things that didn't. The corner boys had a language of their own, they said *fuck* and *cunt* and *gee*. And I was fair game. Hadn't many of them gone to school to my mother? Didn't they know my father well?

News had its own way of travelling, no matter how people tried to spancel it, and once it was travelling the corner boys would ambush it along the way and take what they wanted and send it off again with a different spin.

They knew most of what was happening around the village and what they didn't know they had their ways of finding out.

The months of my mother's pregnancy passed, each with its own step, its own promise. So close to the moment, closer, closer, so close, so close to life. Arriving in the dark night. Not arriving. Here and not here. The limp body on the sheet beside her. This was all there was. The doctor and the midwife redundant. That terrible silence where the cries should have been. An audience expecting sound but no sound comes. The tiny lungs refuse to rise and fall. There's nothing, nothing at all. A lifeless child, a torso. That's all. Blue white. Dead. There, the word is out. Dead. So dead, as if there are degrees of death. There are no degrees, no easy deaths for children. And no easy acceptance. Just death. It's as ordinary as that.

What was there to say that night when the child was found and lost? What word could offer any solace when the only sound that mattered was smothered by absence?

In my imagination I try to listen for the hush in my parents' bedroom, a silence, an awful stillness insinuating itself into everything.

And was it worse the second time and the third? Did the silence deepen and smother everyone and everything? Did sorrow give way to despair?

Sometimes, when I'm alone in my own house, when the family is away and the day is dying, I sit in the kitchen and try to understand how my father must have felt, sitting in the kitchen on the Low Terrace. Hearing the voices from the bedroom, Dr Dyer and Nurse Stanley urging my mother to push. *Just one more push, just one.* The cajoling and encouraging, the *yes, yes* of the arrival and then the change of tone that tells him something is wrong. Was it worse for him the second and third times?

Even in my imagination, even when I think I have some sense of how the house felt then, I never try to venture into my parents' bedroom, never try to picture my mother there because I have no inkling of what she felt.

There was nothing she wouldn't talk about when she was alive. She loved conversation but she never mentioned any of this to any of us, not once, so I don't dare intrude, even in imagination, on her loss.

A summer evening, at the tail-end of a school holiday and we've already been to the Back River, pretending to swim or trying to learn. Joe Whelan and myself cross that small wilderness of grass and poppies and vetch. We squeeze through the gap in the ditch and launch ourselves out into the field, darting among the men playing football. Men, middle-aged and young, with their trousers tucked into their socks, their shirts – already soaked from days spent thinning or weeding beet – flapping as they rise high to field the ball.

There never seems to be any organised pattern to their training. Instead, ten or a dozen of them crowd in around the goalposts and another group congregate in the centre of the field and the hours pass in kicking the ball in and out.

Their voices ring.

Anyone got the lend of a left boot?

The ball lofts lazily, beautifully between the posts.

Jasus, how come you can't do that and you playing?

A shot screws away off the edge of a rubber boot and dribbles hopelessly wide.

You wouldn't kick shite.

We're free now, free of everything. We run barelegged into clumps of nettles, chasing the wild, wide balls that fly from errant feet. For the few seconds that we have the ball we're the centre of attention.

Here, here. Here! Kick it here. Good man. Me, me, me! C'mon to be fucked, kick it.

And then there's unexpected weight of the tightly laced leather, hard against open sandals.

You call that a kick?

Laughter, catcalls, the ball ballooning into the blue sky, men jumping together between the posts and then it's pumped out again.

Behind the goalposts old men play meggars, men who balance on toes like hob-nailed ballerinas, leaning slightly forward to pitch the horseshoes. There's a fragrance of Woodbine smoke. The gentle clink of the horseshoes settling around iron bars. Quiet words that we can't hear.

It was easy then, to leave things behind, to run from one adventure to another. To ramble from the Back River, through the Rocks, up Rice's Hill, home, across the football pitch, down through the Cavalry field to the Abbey.

But now there's no escape, no exorcism, from the attitude that said, *We're all children of God*, the same attitude that refused to allow these children inside the gates of Christian rest.

I think about that and I keep coming back to the corner boys, the men who knew more about the truth than I ever gave them credit for. I imagine I hear them laughing, berating me for my naiveté.

There's nothing new in what you're finding out for yourself, nothing particular about your case. Weren't we all through it in our own time? If it wasn't burying children, it was baptising them or getting their fathers and mothers married in the nick of time. Or getting them married at all.

Their guffaws clack and clatter like a death rattle across the village square.

Many's the morning we'd see them sneakin' into the sacristy for the quick job. One quick job leads to another, wasn't that the way of it? By Jasus, that was the way of it. Some things could be done and some things couldn't. It all came down to spon- dulicks in the end. But, sure, that was always the way. Who do you think was in the front row in the church? Who got called up to read off the altar at Christmas and Easter? Teachers, doctors, shopkeepers. The same ould shite, day in, day out.

Old Mother Hubbard went to the cupboard to get her poor doggie a bone, but when she bent over Rover drove her, for he had a bone of his own. That was always the way. The less you had the more they fucked you. Are you only learning that now? Bit late in the day isn't it?

But some things they wouldn't give way on at all, like burying unbaptised children in the graveyard. Even money couldn't get them in.

And I imagine my mother standing at the kitchen window, washing the dinner things, glimpsing us through the lacework of flowering-currant and apple branches. Watching us, her other, living children, crossing the scented wilderness where they were buried, the several little bodies. And she must have thought back to the nights when they were born.

And, sometimes, when the wind blew at two or three in the morning, she must have woken and lain awake, listening. Just that.

In spite of everything, life went on. The corner boys stood at Cope's wall and sucked the life out of Sweet Afton butts. And talked. Eyeing the young girls as they passed back and forth along the street.

In spite of everything, life went on. And death.

Life came out of the black winter nights.

Out of the hurried fumbling against five-barred gates after dances. Out of the slow and gentle fondling that was subdued against the ears of other children in already overcrowded rooms.

Life leaked out of the hot summer nights on Rice's Hill.

Children were born in and out of love. And, anyway, who was to say what was love and what was lust and what habit or necessity?

And wherever life went, death stalked it. All over the parish. Not afraid to come and stand brazenly outside the gates of newly born children. Death didn't give a fuck. Neither did the corner boys but they, at least, knew the times when they should keep their mouths firmly shut.

Standing beside my mother's grave, the family grave, on the morning of her burial, I tried to remember the sound of her voice and I couldn't.

Now, I try again and I imagine I hear the soft West of Ireland lilt that never took on the harder, flatter accent of Kildare. And, when I find the intonation, I let it find its voice.

Stillborn. Still. Still … still. As still as night. No, more still. As still as dawn. As still as that awful moment before the birds convulse into another day. As still as that.

I see the crumpled body, incapable of breath, inert and mute. And I hear a voice that seems to come from the other end of the Low Terrace. Then I recognise that voice as my own. And my waiting and my loss come out as one long, wild, tormented cry.

I myself listen now, and the emptiness that surrounds me in the house seems to tremble around the emptiness that's at the core of that cry. And the voice again.

And then the stillness drifts back and I can hear Jack moving in the kitchen. I know that, whatever he's doing, he's listening for me. Then I hear him step into the yard outside. I hear the bolt shot back from the shed door. Hear him empty nails and screws and bits and pieces from one of his wooden boxes on the shelves. The bolt shoots home again and he's back inside the kitchen, searching awkwardly in a drawer for a half-torn sheet in which to wrap our infant child.

I'm not there when the child is placed inside the wooden box that is his coffin. Not there when Jack folds the sheet around the tiny hands, winds it round the arms and legs that never moved. I'm not there when the little face is shrouded, the vacant features covered for the first and last time.

Instead, I lie in the bedroom where he was conceived and born and lost.

I think of the christening robe, carefully wrapped in tissue paper. Carefully wrapped, so carefully. But I'm not there when the infant is swathed. I can only imagine because we will never talk of this again. His existence will never touch our tongues, not even late at night when talk is intimate. Not even in old age. Instead we will bury the words in that nail box, wrap up our confusion and rejection in the half-torn sheet and see it out the door. No church, no hymns, no words, no blessing.

In my head, the church doors and graveyard gates stayed open. In my head, there was delivery from the worst part of my baby's death – the rejection. From the misery of the closed door, the locked gate, the unopened grave. In my head, I heard the neighbours praying in their kitchens.

Our Father, they said, Who art in heaven, hallowed be Thy name, Thy kingdom come, Thy will be done on earth as it is in heaven. Give us this day our daily bread and forgive us our trespasses as we forgive those who trespass against us. And lead us not into temptation but deliver us from evil. Amen

But that was only in my head.

Outside, in the first damp and dripping light, he took the spade from the little shed. The spade with the shining blade, the spade with which he turned and straightened every drill in spring.

Day broke over us.

Day broke over my parents. It broke through the clefts between the curtain and the wall, leaking into the room where my mother lay, worn out by labour and loss. It broke more completely over my father where he bent and dug a grave for their child, in the fallow ground near the bottom ditch. The piece of ground he hadn't got around to tilling, left for another year. Left, perhaps, in the expectation of something just like this.

But, at least, he had that piece of ground. The generosity of the County Council garden allowed a final resting-place for that child and, in time, the other children for whom the church could find no room, the unbaptised who were unwelcome in the clay of a Christian burial ground.

In the watery light, my father dug, his spade cutting cleanly into the clay, laying aside the sods, opening the deep earth just enough to make the necessary space for a short life. And when the grave was dug he went back inside and took the wooden box from the kitchen, one big hand underneath and one on top. Gravedigger, undertaker, mourner. And father burying a child.

Word spread. People heard. These things become known in villages.

The schoolmistress lost a child.

And not the first!

And not the first to lose one.

Everyone knew loss at first- or second-hand.

Coming so late from dances that it was early, young men and women had all, at some time, met men on bicycles, small packages on the carriers, and spades tied like rifles along the crossbars. Men heading down Mullaghcreelan Hill or out by Prumplestown, to lay their infant children in the misty corners of fields or within the ruined walls of derelict churches or in the untilled soil of fairy raths. Village men who lived in houses on the street, houses without gardens.

Where else were they to bury them?

They all knew loss. They could fathom it at a hundred yards. They'd stop their cod acting, fall silent on the Barrack Road, raise their caps in salute, in sympathy. Stand back, the wet nettles and the July poppies spilling dew onto their suits and dresses. They'd stand back and let the dead pass. They all knew loss, recognised its face in old and young.

A long time ago, before my parents' house was built, when the ditch at the end of our garden was just a ditch between two fields, someone bent and wove the branches to make a living fence that grew and strengthened every year.

And then, in the Forties, the Low Terrace was built, the question mark of houses between Keatley's field, the Cavalry field and the football pitch. Our garden was still protected by the ditch and, over the decades that followed, we played in that garden, pushing old car tyres up and down the paths, swinging from the apple branches, playing cowboys in the gooseberry and blackberry bushes, crawling, undetected, through potato drills. Kerr's Pinks and British Queens in flower were our camouflage. And while we played, my father went about his work.

He loved that garden. It was all set out to his pattern. Outside the back door was a small patch of grass with a big swing, a boat that could be crewed by five or six children at a time. Then a hedge of flowering currant and, beyond that, the fruit bushes and the apple trees. Then lawn, crowns of rhubarb, drills of vegetables and below them, inside the woven ditch, the wilderness where we sometimes played. That wilderness of poppy, primrose, coltsfoot, oxeye, sorrel, cowslip and high, blown, brown grasses, the wilderness where the lost children were buried. There they lay, inside the ditch, the children at the garden's end.

On spring nights or when autumn was drawing in, I'd walk down there on some pretence. After I'd hung out the washing or gathered up the bits and pieces scattered by the living children. And I'd stand and listen but they never spoke.

I see her standing there, the sun long gone. All the back gardens fallen silent. The clay settling back after the feathered pounding of the heavy horses and the clean carving of the plough. The smell of the earth in the air, recreating the other times and another smell of earth turned over.

I watch her standing there. I listen with her and I know the children buried there are listening, too. Just as they listened, year on year, to our mad laughter, our childish plans and childish fiascos. They listened while we played among the weeds and wildflowers above their heads and never spilled our secrets.

Ghost-children who never ventured beyond that wilderness, never came tentatively at night to touch the apple flower, never knelt to taste the strawberries.

We played on their graves.

And my parents lived with and without them. With the fruitlessness, the loss of life, the lack of love that denied everything.

So many children, there and everywhere, their young bones twisted in the roots of hedges, cut by the shale of ruined churches, asleep in quiet fields or washed by the waters on riverbanks.

The years passed while our brothers, sisters melted into the earth. We went on living, not knowing.

Christmases came, bringing nothing less than peace, goodwill and hope for every child. A New Year and another New Year and the children's frozen forms were there below the crusted wintry snow.

Sometimes, in January, I'd sit at the kitchen table. Outside the door, snowdrops dripped and the brave heads of daffodils and crocuses needled the ground, no more than that.

Inside, purple irises and hyacinths, the colour of lilac.

I'd sit there, waiting for spring, knowing it comes with or without us. It came without them.

So I'd assemble the facts as best I could, spilling them out like negatives, phantom-figures from another life.

Except these figures have no lives of their own. The children I saw had skin so frail it shone like angels. But they had no lives of their own.

What I saw, when I held those images to the lamp of memory, were tiny bodies, light as shadows, on the makeshift lining of makeshift coffins, in the half-light of yet another lifeless morning. They had no past, no hope, no ambition. They had no life. They were lifeless, inanimate, inert. Life less.

Sometimes, late of a summer's evening, the corner boys would hunker down over a game of pitch-and-toss at the back end of Cope's sheds, straining over the pair of flipped coins, no longer sure in the twilight what was heads or harps.

And they might half-admit, mumbling, leaving phrases and sentences unfinished, to a part of what they felt. It was never any clearer than that. Or, the odd time, when the litany was said at the end of the rosary, they might allow their minds to ramble to another litany. Not the triumphal register of saints ascended but a porous catalogue of loss.

But life went on, there were other crises, other tragedies. Young girls got pregnant and the corner boys knew everything.

No stoppin' them.

Up she flew!

And where do you think? The long grass behind the chapel in broad daylight. Ha, ha. The PP met them and they snakin' around by the bell.

Marriages and threatened marriages.

'I'll marry her', the young fellow says. *'Over my dead body'*, says the ould lad. He walloped the young fellow.

He was never behind the door when it came to dishin' out the rough stuff.

Boyfriends disappeared.

Up she flew!

The corner boys missed nothing.

The years were marked in school-time. First Communions. Confirmations. Cathechism exams. Scholarship exams. And we outgrew the house on the Low Terrace. My parents arranged a swap with another family.

The packing and cleaning and throwing-out and retrieving because something *might come in useful*. The goodbyes, as if we were moving to another town.

That last night, when everyone was asleep, I walked down between the apple trees, across the summer lawn, between the potato drills he'd left ready for the next family. And I stood under the full moon and I started to pray for the children, as I did every night. But the prayers wouldn't come.

All I could do was to remember those lost babies, dead at birth. Unblessed. Buried here at sunrise, deep, too deep to be disturbed, while I lay in the pale bedroom, waiting for the last rasp of the spade in the clay.

And, in the moonlight, I looked over my shoulder for their shadows, for the forms of growing children, flitting between the trees, begging just ten more minutes before it's time to go inside.

I'd willingly have given it but it wasn't in my gift to give anything. Not life, not hope, not a Christian burial. There was nothing I could do. So, I gave them my blessing, my baptism, benediction, Eucharist and consecration.

*And then I left them there and went back inside the house
and lay awake all night.*

A dry day in July, I'm six years old, when we move house
across the football field to the High Terrace. We trek back-
ward and forward across the 150 yards. We meet O'Briens
coming in the opposite direction with their furniture.

The new house has a stairs, three bedrooms, a kitchen,
a sitting room and a bathroom.

Later that summer my father builds a garage and a flat-
roofed back-kitchen and a wall along the front of the
garden. It's all excitement then.

New neighbours on both sides. New names to
remember. Hunts; O'Connells; O'Neills; Mulhalls; Kellys;
Jank Kellys; Hennessys; Mahers; Healys; Jenkinsons;
Kanes; Dowlings; Hickeys; Deverills; Byrnes.

And the corner boys still have their say.

I hear they're on the move.

*The higher up the monkey climbs, the more you see of his
behind!*

It all came out, the whole sad story, in the days after my
mother's death. My father told me the bare facts. Still-
births.

No point in dwelling on it, he said and that was that. But
it kept coming back to me and I kept coming back to it.
And it returns to me every time I remember the Low
Terrace.

I go back to the Low Terrace now, and when I turn the
car at the bend between Byrne's and Lawler's, the first
thing I see is our house. There between Hickey's and
Whelan's. That's where we played. Chasing the high ball

into Kinsella's where I grew up, where Mammy K and Nan were mothers to me.

This place is teeming with memories of happiness. The roadway rings with laughter. If I dared sit on Howe's wall, I'd be back again in that time. I'd see Joe Whelan and myself. Blood brothers. Laughing at some outrageous six-year-old plan.

The Angelus bell is ringing across Keatley's field and Harry Kinsella pushes through the gap in the blackthorn at the end of the Terrace, whistling his way home from work.

But it's different now. I know now there were other blood brothers, sisters. And this is where they would have played or, at least, where their funerals should have passed, where their existence could have been given recognition. This is where we would have remembered them. This is where their names would have been mentioned years afterwards. I find myself searching for those names and faces.

And sometimes, when I hear my father singing a snatch of some old song, I remember the house and the garden and the way it was back there.

Lonely I wandered through scenes of my childhood,
they call back to memory the happy days gone by.
Here's where the children played games in the heather,
here's where they sailed their wee boats on the lake.
Gone now the old folk, the house stands deserted,
no light in the windows, no welcome at the door ...

And I ask myself why I'm trying to dress the facts in language softer than they warrant? To spare the blushes of those who should take responsibility?

Anyway. The times have changed. We live in more enlightened clichés now.

But that kind of talk doesn't drown the silence, can't silence the litany repeated many times, a litany that warrants one more repeating, one more whisper of the never-given names of those dead brothers, sisters here.

I'll say it's to let some sense of spring shine in on them, the lost children, denied all recognition. Buried in ditches, gardens, headlands and fields. Denied their final night inside the walls of church or chapel. Denied a place among the living or the dead. Refused two feet of consecrated ground. Denied birth and existence. Denied even death. The non-existent children of our lives.

There are days when hope is a terrible thing. When whitethorn splashes on ploughed fields and the cherry branches sweep the grass with fists of unthrown confetti. Days when hope is a trout jumping in an evening pool and the furze bursts with the freshest yellow. Days when the birds go on piping endlessly. Sometimes hope is a terrible thing in the face of memory.

My mother is writing a letter. Hardly a day passes when she doesn't write to someone. I'm a small boy and I enquire what her lucky number is. Without thinking, she gives me her birth date.

Later, I'm away to the post office, away for messages, empty milk bottles clattering the rope bag. In the dusk, I give my imaginary horse a favourite name and the number she offered. I race from telegraph pole to telegraph pole against the evening bicycles. I know nothing of absence or loss.

It's autumn but an evening when summer refuses to let go. It's four years since we moved house. I'm playing in the football field and something draws me back to the house on the Low Terrace. I stand at the gap in the ditch and look along the garden. I jump down and walk along the ditch. The richest ditch in these parts, flushed with crab apples, the cherry pitch of sloes that would stick the jawbones of an ass together. Sun through the straw and dark buttonholes of hard green rose-hips. Blackberries filled with the sharpness of winter floods. And everywhere the fans of elderberries on the turn.

This is how it was. These are the facts, scattered like dandelion clocks. I see my parents, time and again in expectation of nativity. And time and time the uselessness, the emptiness, an advent of loss. Their lives a corkscrew turning back on them. They wait and wait but no one comes, no dark-suited, white-collared figure on the early road. There is no welcome for the unbaptised. No resting place, no blessing.

Instead, the midwife stands purposeless in the hallway. My father digs a grave at the bottom of the garden. The lifeless sparrow, which never flew and never fell, is laid in a shroud of sheet at the kitchen door. My mother listens to the shallow hammering from the morning shed, the only bell allowed to ring.

seventeen

The afternoon of January 27, 1993 is dark and wet. It's his father's eighty-fifth birthday and he has a present on the kitchen table. He plans to visit his father at teatime. He has spent the morning and afternoon working on the book.

Just after four, there's a knock on the door. He leaves his writing and goes to answer it. His father is standing on the doorstep.

'Come in,' John says. 'And happy birthday.'

He leads his father through the scullery and into the kitchen. His father sits at the table and John swings the kettle onto the ring.

'Is that the only heat you have?' his father indicates the range.

'No, there's a fire in the sitting room. Come on, I'll show you.'

His father stands quickly, still sprightly, still erect.

John leads him through to where the fire is burning brightly.

'You'd want heat in a place like this,' his father says as they return to the kitchen.

'It's fine.'

'It won't be that fine if you end up with pneumonia out of it.'

'I keep it warm.'

He sets the table.

'I was going to drop over at teatime with this,' he offers the present and card.

'I'll open it later,' his father says and John knows this definitely isn't a social call.

'You'll have a cup of tea?'

'I will.'

He takes a fruitcake from the press and puts it on the table.

'It's not exactly a birthday cake.'

He hears the nervousness in his own voice but he's not sure if his father does.

Wetting the tea, he leaves it to draw on the range. His father is used to railway tea, everyone's tea-leaves thrown into one big kettle, strong enough to trot a mouse on.

'I called up to see the kids when I was in Athy,' his father says.

'Were they in from school?'

'They were. They're great children.'

He can hear the unspoken *in spite of everything*.

'They are.'

'And what's this about living out here. This is no way to live.'

'It's fine.'

'How could it be fine? It's not fine for the children. Children need a mother and a father.'

John hesitates. What to say and how much?

'Children that lose a parent are misfortunate. You have to be sorry for children that lose a mother or father. It's never the same for them. Never. They're always at a loss for what's happened. But where a parent chooses to leave, there's never a call for that. And you needn't expect them to understand. How could they?'

'We're trying to work things out,' John says.

It is, after all, his father's birthday and this is neither the time nor the place for arguing. Besides, there is nothing his wife or he can do or say that will change things. For once, he avoids the temptation to get into a shouting match, to tell his father it isn't his concern.

'Well, the sooner you do the better for all and sundry. It's the children I'm concerned about.'

John believes him. It isn't what other people think or how things look to outsiders. This is a genuine concern for his grandchildren and their happiness.

John pours the tea.

'Did you put tea in the pot at all?' his father laughs. 'Or did you just threaten it?'

'I think it'll be strong enough for you.'

His father pours milk into his cup and throws four spoons of sugar after it, stirring for twenty seconds. Then he tastes the tea.

'It'll do,' he says.

'Will you have a slice of cake?'

'I suppose I might as well. Let the last hour be the hardest.'

They sit and drink and talk about the weather and football and local news. John throws a bucketful of coal – his ration for the day – into the mouth of the range, as though it's something he does every hour. Then he opens the damper and lets his father hear the roar of the burning fire.

'Always keep a good fire in,' he says. 'It's the life of a house.'

He opens his present then and seems pleased.

'Have you any plans for tonight?' John asks.

'They're having a do for me in the pub. A birthday cake and all that.'

He hesitates.

'You're welcome to come if you like.'

'Thanks but the kids are here tonight.'

His father nods and relaxes. He's proffered the invitation. A genuine excuse has been given. Honour is saved all round.

Twenty minutes later, John sees his father to the door. Already, frost is settling on the car. The old man pulls his overcoat around him.

'Be careful when you're driving in for the children,' he says and then clears his throat. 'I'm not trying to interfere, you know. They're lovely children.'

He coughs again.

'Right so,' he says, offering his hand, formally.

John takes it.

'Happy birthday. Enjoy the night.'

He watches as the car is backed out of the yard and driven up onto the road and away towards Castledermot. Then he goes inside and closes the damper on the range. He makes himself a fresh cup of tea and sits at the fire. He's shaking.

Only later that night does he remember that his father's mother died as he was born and that he grew up motherless.

eighteen

'He's what's known as a knight of the road,' my father says.

We're driving in through Hallahoise, on our way home from Athy, my father at the end of a day's work, myself at the end of a day's schooling.

We've just passed Harry Tully walking, hunched, in the opposite direction. Over his shoulder he carries a sack-bag. His hat is brown and worn and the shine from his shabby, threadbare coat catches the evening sunlight.

'Aye, a knight of the road and a harmless man.'

Sometimes, in winter, my father picks him up on the road and takes him to Athy. He travels with us to the railway station and then walks the mile-and-a-half to the County Home, where he spends the darkest, coldest days. On those mornings I sit in the back seat of the Morris Minor. I can't take my eyes off the huge growth on the back of the old man's neck. I wait to hear him speak but he never says a word on those journeys. He climbs in and out of the car in silence. I don't like the smell from his clothes. They smell of clay and sweat and something else.

'He can't help that, my father says. He sleeps in the fields a lot of the time or in Wall's or Green's sheds, so there's not much he can do about it. He's a harmless man. If everyone else was as peaceable the world would be a better place.'

In summer-time we don't see him for weeks on end. My father explains that he spends the warm months walking the roads of Carlow and west Wicklow, sleeping in places he hasn't slept for a year.

Sometimes, during the long school holidays, he reappears, blessing himself, genuflecting arthritically as he passes the church, muttering at us children when we call him names.

I try to keep out of the name-calling. Not because I'm any different from the rest, but because I know that at autumn's end or in early winter, when the frost gets thick, he'll be on the Athy road again. We'll pick him up some morning, at the foot of Mullaghcreelan, and give him a lift to the station. And I'm afraid he'll recognise me and, for once, break his silence.

And, sure enough, as happens every year, the trees go on fire and then drop their ashy leaves. And the last honeysuckle withers in the ditches. And there's a crust of frost on the windscreen in the morning and my father has to swing and curse the starting handle to bring the car to life. And there, at the foot of the hill, resting against the hump-backed parapet is the dark, bent figure of Harry Tully. My father stops the car on the other side of the narrow bridge. I peer through the back window and watch the old man come shuffling like a hedgehog along the road.

He sits heavily into the front seat, resting a moment before he lifts his feet slowly into the car. My father leans across and pulls the door closed. For a while, I can see Harry's cold breath in the warm car and then there's just the heavy sound of his lungs sucking and battling against the season and the day. By the time we reach Grangenolvin, the old man is asleep, his head fallen forward and the growth on his neck bulging against his weather-beaten skin. I smell that smell again but I say nothing. I catch my father's glance in the mirror, as he checks the sleeping knight.

This morning we don't stop at the railway station. Instead, we drive on to the County Home. My father leaves the old man and myself in the car and goes inside the infirmary door. I'm terrified that he'll wake up and say something but he doesn't. My father comes back, with a nurse behind him, wheeling a chair. Together they help the old man out of the car and into the chair. He seems hardly to notice he's been moved.

'I don't like the look of him,' my father says to the nurse.

And then, realising I've heard, he smiles and says, 'But maybe he'll weather the storm, he's a hardy old sailor.'

I know he's making light of the situation, making it easy for me but there's something in his eyes, a look that tells me otherwise.

'Is he going to die?'

My father doesn't answer for a moment. We're driving back down into the town, my father already late for work.

'He might. I'd say he might.'

But he doesn't.

My father rings the hospital the next day and the next.

'He's on the mend,' he tells me.

We're driving up the hill at Mullaghcreelan and the last, low sun is spearing the wintry ditches.

'He's a hardy old fellow.'

And the following spring Harry Tully is on the road again and he raises his hand as we pass. My father waves back.

'Tough as nails,' he laughs.

Years afterwards I smell that smell again. Old age, decay.

nineteen

Deep in the darkness of winter, his first in Hallahoise Cottage, he's sitting in the kitchen, the knuckled showers rapping on the window. The children and he are prisoners in these rooms while the rain sweeps over the valley, swinging in from the Laois Hills before spilling down on their small house.

He has decided on a change of tack. He rings his wife.

'I know things aren't working out that well, when the kids are here to stay.'

'So I gather.'

'I've thought about it a lot, whether it might be time to say something to them, something more definite. About us, about the fact that this is how it's going to be. To put them straight on it.'

He can hear the life of the other house through the silence that follows.

'You don't think that's a good idea?'

'No, I don't. They need to get used to one situation before they face another.'

'They do or we do?'

'They.'

'How would you feel if I took them for four nights this week, to try to get some run of time, of normality with them.'

'If you like.'

'You don't have a problem with that?'

'Not if it works for them.'

'And you don't think we should say something?'

'No. Definitely not.'

He collects the children from school and drops them back to school in the morning. They go to the pictures. They go shopping. They watch television together. He helps with their homework, they share the preparation of the evening meal.

Yet, in spite of his efforts, they're becoming strangers to each other, his pain still bruising and wounding their lives, their uncertainty rendering them speechless. The best they can do is to occasionally argue their corner, to be grateful for the small mercies of days when his blackness lifts to a temporary rationality.

He longs for the warmth of intimate conversation.

In late January, he reaches a breaking point.

He comes home from a shopping expedition to Carlow. It's a Saturday evening, and there's nothing but blackness about him. He cooks a meal and sets three places at the table – one for himself and one for each of the children – after which he lays out three meals and they sit at the table. Or rather he sits there. The children are away for the weekend, gone with their mother to visit friends. He sits at the table, eating slowly, watching the children's food go cold. He is dining quietly, peacefully with his absent children. Dining as he'd like to dine with them. Later, he drives to Athy, back to the house that was home. He has a key, he's feeding the dog while the family is away. He lets himself in and, without turning on the lights, goes into one of the children's rooms, gets into bed and lies there all night, just to smell that child smell from the pillow, just to reassure himself, to remind himself that once he was part of a normal life.

twenty

Today is the day I'll marry Nan Kinsella. I've known her for as long as I can remember and she's known me all my life. She and her sisters and her mother, Mammy K, have been minding me since before I can remember. They live just three doors away from us, on the Low Terrace. They tell me that when I was just a few weeks old and my mother went back to teaching, they came and looked after me in our house.

My mother tells me a different story. She says that's the way it was supposed to be but Kinsella's *were never early-to-bed or early-to-rise people.* So, each morning, one of the girls arrived to look after me. But once my mother had left for school they took me the thirty yards to their own house and kept me there. Then, at twenty to three, mother and daughters descended on our house, gave it a once over and had me shining and ready and the kettle boiling by the time my mother got in from work. That went on for a couple of months until, in the end, they gave up the pretence of minding me at home and every morning, from the day I could first walk, I toddled across the street to their house and stayed there until my mother got home.

Often, even now, I go to Kinsella's in the morning and don't leave till bedtime.

Kinsella's is another home to me. Nan minds me, now that the other girls have gone to work in England. And she rescues me from punishment. Whenever I'm in trouble I run to Kinsella's and stay there until the danger has passed. And I never have to take my shoes off at the door. And Nan and Mammy K always smile when they see me. Nan is my friend.

Kinsella's back garden is our long playground, sloping away from the house and down to the edge of the Cavalry field. It's always a wilderness, never dug and sown the way our garden is. We can get lost there in the summer, when the grass is long and yellow and dry. And, when it's teatime, we often find an elephant hiding in the sorrel, waiting to take us home.

On winter days, when my mother wouldn't think of letting me out, Nan and I set off on adventures to the snowy wastes of the Antarctic.

Risking life and limb, Nan says. Whatever that means. We skate on the frozen dyke at the bottom of the garden, in the shelter of the ditch. And, when the rain comes and the thaw sets in and the garden is too wet, we make a tent under the kitchen table, taking blankets from the bed to block out the world. And Nan borrows her brother Harry's bicycle lamp and we steal biscuits when Mammy K isn't looking and we forget about the world outside. Nan tells me stories and she listens to mine.

And then it's summer again and we can go out in the garden.

It's summer today and Nan and I are getting married. She looks beautiful, more beautiful than I've ever seen her before. She's wearing a bright summer dress and she's carrying a bouquet of wild flowers that she picked herself. And she has flowers in her hair. I'm wearing sandals, shorts and a clean white shirt. Mammy K is the priest and she says all the words. Nan is smiling and she says, *I do.* And then I say, *I do* and I feel happy.

Afterwards, Nan takes two apple tarts from the oven, a big one and a little one. Mammy K puts a candle on the smaller one and lights it.

Now, there's a fine wedding cake.

We blow the candle out and cut the tart and eat it and drink red lemonade and we're laughing and the sky stays blue, even after the sun goes down, right up until darkness falls. And then my new wife walks me home and leaves me at our door and kisses me goodnight, a soft kiss on my forehead.

But a wedding doesn't make a marriage and a day is not a life and our marriage doesn't last. A few weeks afterwards, Nan follows her sisters to Birmingham and a life I know nothing about. And I go back to school. But she remains faithful, she never marries anyone else.

twenty-one

There's no one incident. It's not the bleakness of winter. Spring is all about him but he's obsessed with the question of whether terror is a form of insanity. He's terrified. He's functioning but he's terrified by the possible consequences of his own life.

Terrified by the enormity of the change in that life.

Terrified by the weight of obligation. He can't see how he's ever going to lead a normal life or relate, in any depth, to other people.

Terrified by the future, and what's expected of him. The thought of taking responsibility for the welfare of two children is beyond his comprehension.

Terrified at the possibility of never having a relationship again and, at the same time, terrified of the commitment such a relationship will require.

All these terrors trail other, smaller fears in their wake. Fears that, in normal circumstances, he could easily deal with.

He worries obsessively about the children.

They're due to ring at six and when they don't, he panics at five-past. Rings them three or four times in an evening, simply to hear the sounds of their voices, to know they're all right.

The rain is elbowing down between the cottage and the box hedge, with all the bitter cut of March. He carries a sack of seed potatoes and the spade from the garage. The garden is already prepared. He has dug the ground and made the drills and laid the manure in them. He stoops over the drills, one leg on each side, dropping the seed potatoes onto their beds of cow dung. Rain hops off the shoulders of his coat, slapping down and soaking the backs of his legs. He finishes a drill and turns to plant the next one. A passing cyclist lifts his head out of the mouth of the wind and shouts, 'God bless the work'.

Spring gives way to early summer and its sunshine rituals. Games of cricket and football in the brilliant, bluebell garden; games of hide-and-seek in dusky evenings; walks up the hill; meals with the windows wide open to the night and moths staggering in from the heat outside.

A Saturday afternoon of madness but this is a different kind of madness altogether. They paint the outside doors.

His daughter walks from back door to front door, surveying each, and then returns, shaking her head.

'Dad, I don't think we'll get away with this!'

'Let's wait and see. Let's wait until we get used to it.'

The bright warm, welcoming red on the colour card has become a loud, shocking scarlet on the doors.

They live with the colour for forty-eight hours, long enough for it to dry, long enough for it to blind the morning sun. Then they find a deeper red that doesn't scream.

A weekend in late May, he borrows a scythe from Noel Lambe and cuts the long grass in the back garden. The sun is hot and the sky is clear and they work through the afternoon, stopping only for drinks. He cuts in straight lines, from the fence at the field to the garage wall and back again. The children work a line away from him, raking and collecting the fallen yellow grasses. They lay each armful in a circle and build from there a cock of hay that rises like a totem pole in the garden. They finish as the radiant moon is rising over Fraughan Hill, beginning its journey across the sky. Their work done, they sit, backs against the cocked hay, eating and drinking and talking about what it must have been like in these fields a hundred years before. There are no arguments or tears or tantrums. They fall silent and he imagines they share the same unspoken wish that it may be ever so.

But these days are few and far between, too delicate to tamper with. Even the brightest afternoons and the happiest times have shadows hanging around the edges. At his best, in the days when he remains on an even keel, neither the children nor he can ever be sure that things won't turn upside down. Something as vague as memory or possibility can change his mood. If one of the children is being troublesome his tolerance level is low. If they squabble, he's likely to turn a molehill into a mountain and a three-minute disagreement becomes an hour-long rant that ends in tears and regrets and apologies and promises and a deepening cloud of distrust hanging over everything. Life has become a series of words like *still* and *again*.

twenty-two

My father is sitting at the supper table and I'm playing in
the cubbyhole under the stairs. I have my collection of
cardboard-box radios and I'm quietly repairing them,
turning sheets of newspaper into valves and switches and
tying them together with short pieces of string. My father
is talking about something he saw that day. He's talking
about life as a rhyme of counted magpies.

One for sorrow …

I pretend to go on playing but I'm listening to his
words. I don't understand everything he's saying but I
understand enough to see the picture they paint, a picture
that's as cold and final as death. I see a man, in a dark blue
coat, standing stout in the prow of a boat. Rain is lashing
down between the bridge and the church in Athy. It's a
dull and hollow day and darkness is already falling and the
guards are dragging the river.

twenty-three

Even though he's back living in his own parish, among his own people, he still feels as ill-at-ease and unsure of himself as he has ever done. He does his shopping in the village, stops to talk to people in the supermarket. He passes the time of day with them in the street. They meet at local plays. He falls into conversation with people he grew up with as they follow a hearse to Coltstown cemetery.

'He went off quick in the end.'

'He did.'

'He was a decent skin. You must've taught his kids.'

'I did, yeah.'

'Jasus he faded to nothing the last few months.'

'Right.'

'Skin and bone.'

He can't honestly say that he knows these people or that they know him. There seems no way of changing this state of affairs. And, anyway, digging deep and uncovering truth is fraught with the danger of discovering that what you saw is not what you get. Bad enough that pleasant people become disagreeable when you really get to know them, worse still that prejudices turn out to be unfounded, when intolerance is undermined, when old enemies turn out to be decent people.

twenty-four

I'm five years old. I'm being pushed in our pram. The pram is tall, well-sprung and rounded with a high hood that can be lowered or raised. It makes a great stagecoach. This is the same pram that my brother and sister and I were pushed in as babies but now it has served its purpose and we use it for amusement.

My sister is pushing the pram with one hand and rolling an old car tyre with the other. The road is deserted and the day is warm. It's summer. There are dandelions shining everywhere, even on the high ruins of the old town wall. They are yellow lights in the dark ivy.

When we reach the ruined wall, at the place where the Low Terrace joins Carlow Gate, the tyre is hidden in the long grass and my sister pushes the pram onto the path and into the village.

This is the same summer when my brother and his friends take the tin bath from our shed and carry it across the fields to the Mill Pond. They ask me if I want to come along. My father is at work. My mother is away for the day. I trudge along behind them. Two of them carry the tin bath between them. One of them carries a rope. Another carries the tube of a car tyre. When we get to the pond they tie the rope to the handle of the bath. Then they put me into the bath and launch it out onto the fathomless Mill Pond. It floats. I squat on the cold tin and journey away from the shore, as far as the rope will go. They take it in turns to pull the bath backwards and forwards, with and against the current. They take it in turns to stand on the bank with the car tube, their lifeboat should the bath capsize. Afterwards, we trek back home again. My brother warns me not to tell my mother about the *adventure*. They put the bath back in the shed. The tube goes back wherever it came from.

Later that night, I tell my mother about our journey, about being a pirate and our great endeavour. At first she doesn't believe me and then it dawns on her that this is too detailed to be an invention and then all hell breaks loose. My father is called in. My brother is in the wars.

There are four tyres in our garden. One comes from the Ford Prefect my father drives, two are slightly larger and no one seems to know where the fourth came from. Each tyre is a horse but only two have names – Orange Layer and Cho-Cho.

Sometimes my sister plays with them and sometimes Joe Whelan and I run along the garden paths, pushing them with our hands. When we weary of that, we sit on them, talking cowboy talk.

'Howdy pardner.'

'Howdy.'

'Much trouble at the saloon last night?'

'Nope.'

'Seen Jessie James riding by a while back.'

'Which way did he go?'

'Thata way.'

'Let's go shoot him dead.'

'Shure thing.'

And sometimes, when there's no one else to play with, I ride my horse to the bottom of the garden and talk to Jesse James. We've shot him a hundred times, but he's a survivor and, anyway, I secretly admire him. Mostly, I'd rather be in his gang than in the Sheriff's.

When my sister plays, she insists we park the tyres around the huge swing in the garden and picnic there. No running, no horse riding, no question of cowboys: it has to be Mr and Mrs this and that.

And, sometimes, the tyres are turned into props in concerts in the garage. I get walk-on parts but, to me, I'm just another prop.

One afternoon, I get bored with my silent role. Instead, I ease one of the tyres from behind a table and roll it through the newspaper curtains. The conscript boys in the audience love it. My sister is not amused. My mother is not impressed. I'm sent to bed.

Afterwards, when I peep out under the sun-lit bedroom curtains, I have the comfort of seeing Orange Layer waiting in the shadow of the flowering currant, ready for another great escape.

twenty-five

When the arguments start, as often as not, they start without a reason. Probably because there seldom are any reasons worth remembering. Rather, the anger that explodes is just a part of his ongoing frustration.

He's making an apple tart. It's a Saturday afternoon. The children are playing noisily, harmlessly, racing from bedroom to sitting room, chasing each other. The sounds of their voices are somewhere beyond the closed door. The thump of their shoes on the carpeted floors does not really encroach on his thoughts. And then there's a loud bang and a silence and a wailing and his son pounds through the kitchen doorway, his sister hot on his heels.

'She knocked me down.'

'I did not, he slipped.'

'You did, you liar, you pushed me.'

He goes on, rolling the pastry, saying nothing.

His silence doesn't seem to be doing the trick. His son's wailing goes up an octave.

'She's always pushing me, she's always trying to hurt me.'

He hates that word, *always*. It grates on him.

His daughter's eyes begin to fill with tears.

'If you can't play together, why don't you do something else, one of you play outside?'

'Why don't you tell her to stop pushing me, you're always taking her side.'

That word again.

'And why don't you shut up or just keep to hell out of one another's way? Why don't you keep out of my way? Why does every game have to end in a squawking match? Is it not possible for you ever to play together without fighting? Why can't you just behave yourselves?'

Suddenly, he's the one who's shouting. He can feel the anger rising inside him. Is he ever, in his father's phrase, going to have peace or ease?

'Do I always have to sort things out between you. Why the hell can't you spend forty-eight hours in the house without screaming at each other? Can't you see, don't you know I'm trying to make something for you, especially for you, are you determined to ruin my best efforts? For Christ's sake, what else do you want from me?'

He brings the rolling pin down heavily on the table. It smashes and the noise silences the children but it doesn't silence him. His voice rises above the echo of the broken roller.

'If you can't behave yourselves, just get out of the house, out! Go on, go! Out, get out, out, out, out, just get out of my sight!'

He hurries them towards the back door and into the garden, banging the door behind them. They stand on the step for a moment, tears on both their faces.

He goes back and picks the pieces of the rolling pin from the floor and throws them across the room.

'Fuck, fuck, fuck!'

He's sick, he's angry, he wants to turn back the clock, to sort things out, to sit them down, to explain, to be a proper parent, to stop being like this again and again. He promised himself this wouldn't happen this weekend. This was going to be a good weekend. Nice meals, the things they liked, a good film on TV, bags of sweets hidden in the press for later. A weekend they'd be sorry to see end.

'Bollocks! What is the fucking point?'

Outside, the children have moved away from the door. He watches them climb into the field across the lane, he knows they're running away. He peers through the net curtain. They walk between the trees and stop. Despite the sun, the afternoon is chilly. They stand in their T-shirts, in the shadow of the hedge, glancing back towards the cottage, waiting for him to come looking for them. But he stays in the heated kitchen and does nothing. He wants to go to them but he's drained and close to tears himself. He goes back to the table and fills the base and rolls out the remaining pastry, using a bottle instead of the broken pin. He puts the tart in the oven. Only then does he return to the window. The field is empty. They're hiding, he thinks, so he cleans the table and washes the dishes. But what if, what if they've taken it one step further? What if they've gone out on the road and are walking towards Athy?

He opens the back door and races onto the lane. The sun is dipping below the tree line, the May afternoon turning chilly. No sign of them in the field, no sign on the road, what if someone has stopped and picked them up? Turning, he runs back towards the car. Only then does he see the white shirts, deep in the shadows of the garage.

'Come in.'

They stand their ground.

'Come in now, you'll get pneumonia.'

They shuffle out of the shadows, afraid again, and follow him inside.

'Sit there,' he tells them, indicating the armchairs on each side of the range.

Their faces are dirty, stained with well-rubbed tears.

He knows what he wants to do. He wants to hug them, take them in his arms and tell them he's sorry because he is sorry. Tell them he loves them because he does love them. But what's the point, he's done it all before, gone through the explanations and the promises and all to no avail. So, instead, he launches into another rant.

'This has got to stop, you can't go on behaving like this anymore. I can't take this nonsense. You have to learn to behave yourselves. Either that or keep away from each other. But I'm not having you coming out here week after week and fighting and squabbling. I'm just not having it. I won't take it. That's it. No more.'

As he thumps the table, he sees them jump. It's getting dark outside, there's nowhere left to run.

'Now stay there. Stay there until you get warm again. Don't move.'

He goes into the bathroom and when he comes back his eyes are dry and the children are still in their chairs.

'I'm not taking this,' he says another weekend. 'I'm not putting up with this any more. You come out here, you fight, you spend your time just making my life a misery. That's it. Three fights in one day. Get your stuff, you're going back to Athy. I can't take this any more.'

It's ten o'clock on a Friday night. He waits in the kitchen while the children silently collect their clothes and books and then he bundles them into the car.

Driving the six miles to Athy, the lecture goes on. He shouts, they sit ashen-faced.

'If you have no respect for me, if you can't behave in a civilised way, then you can't stay in the house. I'm not prepared to listen to a weekend of fighting. So you can go somewhere else and do it. Maybe your mother can put up with it, I can't, you're driving me round the twist.'

'We're sorry.'

'Sorry! Hah, easy to say sorry. I asked you not to fight. I asked that we have one peaceful weekend and you lasted what? Five hours! Too late for sorry.'

'But we are.'

'It's too late.'

He turns onto the road where they all once lived only to discover there are visitors' cars outside the house and they can't go home.

Home is the place their mother lives. Home is where their lives have peace and predictability. The cottage was to have been the great adventure, the place they'd come for weekends and enjoyment but now it's the place where every adventure is a nightmare. What they've endured so far is a lucky dip of days when he's capable of entertaining them and days when he's at the bottom of the mountain and can neither see nor recognise hope.

He hasn't learned to differentiate between righteous anger and self-loathing. Nor has he learned to aim his rage in the right direction and find the proper targets. For that reason, the children bear the brunt of his unhappiness. It's only their love, and their refusal to be cowed by his anger and sadness, that's seeing them through the darker days of this year of strangeness.

twenty-six

It's a gloomy Saturday afternoon, floor-washing, floor-polishing day and, rain or no rain, I'm out on the road until the lino is washed, dried, polished and shone. Sometimes I get that job to do, shining. I tie a cloth around the head of the sweeping brush and smooth it backwards and forwards across the floor. At first, it jars and catches but, bit by bit, the wax polish is worked into the surface and the brush slides easily across the floor and I can see the light catch the gloss.

But not today, today is a busy day, a day for just getting the floors done. I don't know why and I don't ask. Instead, I gratefully pull on my duffel coat and escape into the soft, dusky afternoon.

Winter hangs like a threat over the gardens and houses. The last few sorry dahlias in Howe's are well-rusted. The rain is fine and smells of turf, squatting like smoke on the roof of every house along the Terrace. I call to Whelan's, where Joe is already on his way out to meet me.

At Stanley's wall a clutch of children are playing in the shelter of the bare bushes hanging in from Keatley's field. The wind is coming from the east and there's a patch of dry clay where the last leaves haven't yet fallen from the trees. Joe and I hunker down there with two other boys and we mark a patch for marbles and forget the rain and the cold. The other, smaller children are playing on the road, puddling their boots in loughs of water, their heads bent to watch the ripples that run away from them. The marbles flash and clack. A coal lorry crawls along the Terrace. We look up and then go back to our game. The driver parks the lorry at the other end of the road. The coal-man humps sacks into one of the houses. Children appear from doorways, gathering around the sides of the high, wooden-floored lorry. They duck and dive and chase. We ignore them, the game is too important. The lorry moves down the Terrace, the coal man walking behind it. The driver backs slowly, angling the lorry into the open space near Byrne's gate. The coal man lifts a wet sack of coal and carries it around the side of a house. Someone produces a huge silver ball bearing and gets my marbles in his sights. The coal man comes back and lifts another sack from the trailer and hefts it on his back and disappears again. *Clack.* One of my marbles is taken, flying into the leaves. *Clack.* Another gone.

'That's it,' the coal man shouts, swinging into the cab.

The ball bearing flies again and misses. Now's my chance. I line up a yellow marble in my sights, squatting low. My eye is close to the ground, the clay like a dry desert below me.

Somebody says, *Fuck.*

I close one eye and shoot. The yellow marble flies off the line. One back.

Then *Fuck* again.

I kneel up, turning to sight the orange marble on the angle of the pitch, but there's no one here, the other boys have gone. They're twenty feet away, standing around the tailboard of the lorry. The driver and the coal man have leapt from the cab. I knock the orange marble from its place, put it in my pocket and go to see what's happening. The two men are on their hands and knees beneath the trailer.

Is she broke?

There's a young fellow under it, he was playing in there.

I stand on my toes to catch sight of what's happening but all I can see are the two men, their coats soaked with rain. And then women are running along the Terrace and someone wobbles away on a bicycle for the doctor. And Nurse Stanley is there, her knees wet and dirty as she crawls under the lorry. And a woman is crying but her cries are quiet and dry, not like any crying I've ever heard before. And the driver is squatting beside the tailboard and his face is white and he's saying, *I never seen him, I swear I never seen him*, over and over. And Nurse Stanley and the coal man lift a small boy out from under the trailer. I notice that their faces are wet with rain but the little boy's is dry. There's a bruise on his forehead but otherwise he looks all right. I wait for him to move, to cry, to laugh. I wait for his mother to give out to him.

He never had a chance, somebody says.

twenty-seven

He opts for pragmatism. He will put aside his love affair with melodrama, he will embrace the summer. He has to sort out, once and for all, what the children need from him and give it to them. Practicality is the key. Sort out the parent/children situation and the rest will be easier.

But how does it work, this bond between his children and himself? He has been parent and child and he knows it doesn't simply turn on kindness or favour or good grace. Much of the time it's there in spite of, as much as because of, everything. He wishes he could put his trust in something, find something to guide him. He tries prayer but – even if he believed – he was never taught to think of Jesus as uncertain or perplexed, a man with his head in his hands. Jesus is the man with the answers and if the answers always come to Him, how can He understand someone who hasn't even found the questions? And, anyway, much and all as He suffered, He never had children of His own.

He shares a pleasant meal with the children; they sit, they talk. He irons out the things that irk him, the small things like not tidying up, not clearing the dishes, not doing homework without being supervised, squabbling for no good reason. But, when it comes to the children's turn to have their say, they're silent, apart from something about *not always arguing*.

He tries to tease things out.

'You can say whatever you want to say, just say it. I won't get annoyed.'

Silence.

'Honestly. Just say whatever you want. Do you want me to leave you alone for a while, to talk about it?

Silence again.

When he thinks about it, he realises he's not going to get any further and he sees why.

How can he expect them to take him at his word? This isn't the first time he's set about rectifying the situation. Should he suddenly expect everything to be sweetness and light; does he have any right to believe they'll accept his promises of peace and quiet and rationality and forget the trail of broken promises and rows and disruption he has left in his wake over the months?

'I'll tell you what,' he says, 'if I get through the next week without losing the head, will the two of you talk to me again about this?'

They look at each other and nod slowly but without any great conviction.

twenty-eight

Flamboyant is a word I've heard. I looked it up in the dictionary and it seems to fit but it's not a lot of use to me because, most of the time, I can't remember it and, when I do, I can't pronounce it so it doesn't really count. But *flamboyant* is what he is and, in a time when our lives are grey, this flamboyant man lives a life that's Technicoloured. The fact that he's one of our own, that he grew up locally, went away, and came back a different man, makes him all the more remarkable in our star-struck eyes.

But it isn't just us children who are struck by Peter Murphy's difference. We hear our parents talking. They say *he's made his mark on the village lives* and we know they think the same.

We're snotty-nosed ten-year olds. Half the time some of us are hungry for food, and all of us are hungry, all of the time, for adventure and excitement and the kinds of lives we see on the screen in the picture house.

We're living in 1962. John Kennedy, the Catholic President, is in the White House. TV is something silent, viewed through Cope's shop window on Saturday evenings. Week after week, Rin Tin Tin saves the day.

It is a time when the village streetlights only burn beyond midnight at Christmas. For the rest of the year, late walkers travel in blackness.

You're living in the dark-ages, our teacher tells us sarcastically as he beats us. But he doesn't know and doesn't care how hard we're searching for the sunlight.

An argument runs, among the children I play with— for an entire autumn, winter, spring and most of a summer—about whether or not soccer goalkeepers are allowed to handle the ball, but no one can resolve it with any certainty and we never think to ask an adult. The game is foreign to our lives, and yet it attracts us because it has the magic of something we know nothing about. It isn't until the end of that summer, when Michael O'Neill comes back from his holidays in England, that the argument is finally settled and unfortunate keepers are allowed to stop using their heads as fists and their faces as the last line of defence!

There are little excitements and we latch onto them for importance.

An unmarried girl in the village gets pregnant, the first unmarried mother we've found out about, but she disappears to England before we can enjoy the excitement and scandal, and wonder at her boldness, or fantasise about how exactly it happened and where and when and who with.

One of our gang says he heard a woman on his road is *having an affair.* That sounds like something we should know more about, but neither he nor any of the rest of us know what an affair is so that story dies a death.

Through the summer, we content ourselves with playing football, thinning and weeding beet and following courting couples out the Mill Road.

The real excitements hinge on the comings and goings of Peter Murphy – the extraordinary owner of the local cinema. He's a legend in our lives and his history is the stuff of cowboy adventures. His behaviour shocks and delights us. His daring amazes us.

The story runs through the village that he worked in New York as a taxi-driver and, one day, stuck in rush-hour traffic, with a fare in the back seat, he decided enough was enough. Abandoning cab, fare, job, future, everything, he jumped on a plane and came back to Ireland. Once here, he got a job as a commercial traveller but, and we have this on the best authority, *that was just to keep body, soul and family together*. The real reason for his homecoming was to return to Castledermot and open the Castle Cinema, to bring the outside world into our lives and cast the vagaries of the world before us.

Whether the story is truth or half-truth or legend doesn't matter a damn. Just the thought of it thrills us. He's been to America and, better still, he's come back! We know that when he arrived in the village, he started building a house from pre-cast concrete. People said it would fall down, that it was madness, that the rain would destroy it in a winter. People said he should have been happy with the kind of house his people had before him. People said all kinds of things but the house went up and, when it was finished, he painted it and called it *The White House*. The locals were stunned. The nerve, the cheek, the cheek!

Naming a house!

Only one other house in the village had a name! And naming it after the residence of the President of the United States was a big-headed, ludicrous idea.

'Who the hell does he think he is? It's far from White Houses he was raised.'

'He might have notions now but it won't be long before he's brought back down to earth.'

And we're told, *reliably*, about his appearances around the village during those first summers back in Castledermot. Summers when he went shopping in shorts.

'Mother of Jasus, has he no cop on at all, does he not know where he is and who he is? He's making a laughing stock of himself!'

I overhear my mother say *he has given the exclamation mark a new lease of life.*

But it isn't just the outlandish dress that's getting to people. It's Peter's refusal to live down to the low expectations they have of him. He hasn't fallen on his face, *the curse of God* hasn't struck him down, *The White House* hasn't collapsed and he hasn't lost his job.

'Where's the justice?'

'What the hell is going on?'

And, then, there's the picture-house, except it isn't a picture-house. It's a cinema.

'A mad whore of a notion, a cinema in a village of 400 souls.'

'It'll never work, there's not the people to keep it going, who'd be bothered anyway?'

But it's built and it opens and the people come. A matinée and an evening show on Sunday, evening shows on Wednesday and Friday. And the seats! Woodeners at the front, what else did we expect, but plush seats at the side and the back.

'Madness, they'll be ripped to bits.'

But they aren't. Peter Murphy has standards and he expects the rest of us to accept and respect them when we're on his premises. We don't always rise to those expectations but he refuses to accept anything less for his cinema and his furniture and, in the end, he has his way. We may whistle when the lights go down, we might try to sneak from the wooders to the grander seating at the back, we may stamp and shout when the film breaks down but we won't wreck the place and that's that.

And further shock and horror and scandal are to follow. The back row of seats is taken out and replaced with double seats: *love seats*.

'Ah, Jasus, that's going too far, is it a fuckin' picture house or a knockin' shop? The Parish Priest will have something to say about that; you mark my words, they'll be out in a week.'

But they aren't.

For a time, our attention turns from the screen to the dark recesses of the back row. We're more determined than ever to get out of the wooders and to investigate what exactly goes on in the love seats. We've heard that fellows up there are *running the hand* and girls are *dropping the hand*. We club together and draw straws to send a fully paid-up scout to sit in the dear seats. It costs us half-a-crown but we're left none the wiser. All he sees are the backs of heads and all he hears are *the sound of kissing*.

'What kind of sound?'

'You know, a slobbery sound.'

'Is that all?'

'You'd see more on the Mill Road.'

'You were watchin' the picture, that's what's wrong.'

'I was not. It's too feckin' dark up there.'

Whatever the Parish Priest feels about the new seats, they stay put and hands continue to drop and run and we remain on the wooders in our frustrated ignorance.

And then Peter branches out. Once a week, the wood-eners are removed and dances are held. Posters, for big-name bands, appear in shop windows. The crowds come from as far away as Baltinglass and Athy and Tullow.

'And there's *prostitute*s hanging around outside.'

'What's a prostitute?'

I'm delegated to find out. It's not an easy job. I have to get the house to myself long enough to get the dictionary from the top shelf in the bookcase but I discover Edna O'Brien in the process. I spell out the word and write the definition in the torn-out middle pages of a school copy-book. But I'm not about to give all that effort up without getting as much as I can from it.

'Do you know what a *proboscis* is?'

'No.'

'An elephant's trunk.'

'That's fuckin' great. We really needed to know that.'

'And *prolapse* is to fall down.'

'I'll prolapse you if you don't tell us.'

'It wasn't in it.'

'Ah, shite.'

Disappointment all round.

'No, it was, I'm only coddin'.'

We're huddled in the shelter of the big rock on Rice's Hill. I take the folded sheet from my pocket.

'A prostitute is *a woman who offers herself for in-dis-crim-in-ate sexual in-ter-course, especially for hire. To offer for lewd purposes.*'

'What's indiscrate?'

'Dunno.'

'What's lewd?'

I check the page.

'Indecent, unchaste, depraved.'

'Why didn't you look up indiscrate?'

'I hadn't the time. I could of got caught.'

'Me bollicks.'

A voice from the edge of the circle.

'My brother says a prostitute is a woman that'll let you put your mickey in her for money.'

'Aaaach.'

'He says there's two of them in Carlow —*Stick It Out* and *The Threepenny Man*.'

Friday night, in the safety of the cinema's darkness, we dare each other to shout out the forbidden names.

'You go.'

'No, you.'

'Why don't you?'

'Right, we'll all do it together.'

'One, two, three ….'

'Stick It Out! The Threepenny Man!'

My voice rings out, the only voice. The other three sit silent. In the light from the screen I can see the smirks on their faces. Peter Murphy descends like an avenging angel and I'm outside the door before I know it.

'I won't tell your parents, young man. But you're barred from this cinema for one week.'

At the interval, as the crowd pours out and crosses the street to Paddy Byrne's sweet shop, my three amigos appear, still grinning.

'Ya fuckin' eegit.'

'How long did he bar you for?'

'A week. Youse are shites.'

People buy their sweets and minerals and cross back over the street, handing in their pass-outs at the ticket desk. The doors close and I'm left sitting on Coady's wall. I can't go home until the picture is over. If I do, my mother will want to know why and I'll be in real trouble. So I sit in the fading summer sunlight instead and try to imagine what the big picture is about, try to concoct some great plan of revenge on my companions.

And, then, the cinema doors open. I look up. Peter Murphy has stepped outside for a breather. He walks down to where I'm sitting. I think of running but it's too late now. I wait for his words, for a lecture, a criticism, a warning, blame.

'Isn't that a beautiful evening?' he asks.

His voice is quiet and even, I hear no sound of anger.

'Yeah.'

I'm uncertain.

The light shafts down through the ruins of the Franciscan Abbey.

'America is a wonderful country.'

I nod.

'Especially for sunsets.'

I want to ask him about the taxi story, to ask if there's any truth in it but I don't dare.

'Everyone should travel,' he says, turning and looking at me as if I'm an adult. 'You should travel, when your time comes. When they say it broadens the mind they're right. No harm in being here but when you go away and come back you see things in a different light. Totally.'

There's something in his tone and, for those few minutes, I feel he's talking to me as an equal. It's as though he hadn't thrown me out of the cinema half–an-hour before for being a young pup.

'Yes, travel is a great eye-opener.'

He turns and glances at the cinema and then at his watch.

'Right,' he says. 'No rest for the wicked, must get back.'

And he's gone.

I don't mention the conversation to my friends. Instead, I listen to their versions of what the film was about; they can't agree on anything and it ends in a row but I don't really care. I feel a kind of comfort, and I'm almost grateful that I was thrown out. I convince myself that I've been part of a conversation, been treated as an equal, even though my contribution was a solitary mumble.

Every St Stephen's Day there's a matinée at the cinema – a feast of sweets; Hollywood crash, bang, wallop and a raffle where no one goes home empty handed.

St Stephen's Day is *the* picture day in the year. The Wren Boys count for little with us, the matinée is every-thing. I scramble out of bed sometime mid-morning while the rest of the house is still sleeping. In the sitting room, I breakfast on the handful of Black Magic littering the almost empty box under the sofa. One by the one the rest of the family appears. We have our lunch and then, at half-two, it's time to leave for the picture house.

I stuff my pocket with Lemon's sweets, take a chunk of Christmas cake for the journey and then I'm off. Coming down the road Michael O'Neill and Sean Healy and Liam Mulhall and Joe Whelan rein in their trusty steeds beside mine. We head down the quiet street, the five horsemen of the apocalypse. At the cinema door Frank McDonald, the bouncer, eyes us through, Christmas being a time of amnesty when all is forgiven if not forgotten. Mrs Murphy gives each of us a free raffle ticket and we make our way to our regular places in the wooderners.

The enormous tree which lights the cinema seems higher than any tree has a right to be. It has been erected to the side of the space between our seats and the dear seats. We guess how high it might be. Beneath it, prizes lie wrapped, prizes for the raffle held in the interval between the little and big pictures.

Peter Murphy is at his most awesome on those St Stephen's afternoons – dressed to kill, his bow tie winking. He dominates the stage, pulling tickets from a hat, laughing, telling jokes, entertaining us, distributing presents. We sit in the light of the giant Christmas tree. We wait for our numbers to be called. For some, this is like a second visit from Santa Claus. For others, it's the first and only visit and, for once, the wealth or poverty of any child's family doesn't warp the Christmas spirit. All are equal in this man's eyes. Inside the walls of the Castle Cinema, Christmas is a time of peace, good will and communism.

And after the picture ends, after the screen goes dark, after the lights shatter our fantasies, I head out, cap gun drawn from my newly won holster, six-shooter firing a thousand times. Across the unlit ravine of the School Lane, past the land-drainage yard and Lawler's and Kinsella's and Matt Neill's and home to my own yard where Brandy and Soda are lying, tails lapping, waiting for me to stable my horse for the night.

A Sunday comes, a memorable Sunday, and I'm allowed out to the evening film. I've heard the story about how Peter plays the violin in the break between the little picture and the big one and I don't believe it. But, sure enough, here he is climbing onto the stage and playing the fiddle. And, when the music has finished, he flags the comings week's attractions, one of them *starring Audie Murphy – no relation.*

But I don't believe that either. I know, in my heart of hearts, that this man has to be closely related to the film star. He just has to be. He has the style, the wildness, and the glamour that I know, without knowing why, belongs in Hollywood. And, should he step from the stage into the hot, dusty desert with John Wayne, I won't be surprised. That's where he belongs – racing on horseback across the Red River Valley to save a family in need – not on the wet, badly lit, poverty-ridden streets of Castledermot.

Sometimes, years later, when his name comes up in teenage conversations, Peter Murphy is referred to as *a fuckin' eegit*, which, in its own backhanded, roundabout, primitive way is a compliment. *A fuckin' eegit* is not *a sack*. *A sack* is almost the lowest of the low, just above a *toolbar*. *A fuckin' eegit* dares dreams, is different, can lay claim, in a small village, to a grudging respect and an unspoken esteem. *A fuckin' eegit* is different. *A fuckin' eegit* thumbs his nose at convention, does what the rest of us fear to even consider and scandalises our parents.

And Peter Murphy qualifies on all counts.

But, on an entirely different level, there's a human decency about the man that belies his eccentricity. He knows us, knows who and what we were, and what we have and don't have.

twenty-nine

By the time John moved to the cottage, the pictures had long stopped flickering in the picture-house. After the last reel flittered out, the building went through a brief reincarnation as a discotheque and then another short life as a carpet warehouse. By the early Nineties, it was redundant.

Sometimes, when the children and he are snuggled up, watching the late horror film on a Friday night, half-terrified but not admitting it, he tells them about the Castle Cinema and about the legends people needed to create around Peter Murphy, as if their lives depended on them.

The legend that, on the night his brother's body was taken to the local church, he opened the cinema for business with the immortal lines, *Willie is dead, Peter must live. The show goes on!*

The outrage that followed the cinema's opening for business on Christmas night. This was *going against all that's holy and wholesome.*

But the people who criticised were the people with families. The people with someone to visit, the people who enjoyed the luxury of television – never the people who lived alone and had their visiting done by tea-time, if they had anyone to visit at all. To them, the open doors of the cinema were a godsend.

Another summer evening and they drive, the three of them, on a whim, to Coltstown graveyard. They go to Peter Murphy's grave and read the words that are carved on the plain stone:

> *In memoriam laetam et in dulci jubilo.*
> *Peter E Murphy*
> *Castledermot and Rathgar*
> *Who died 27th May 1991*
> *Musician, Sportsman, Gentleman*
> *In God we trust.*

He remembers all the things the Castle Cinema meant in childhood. One thing is uppermost, the fact that the cinema had promised sex on and off the screen and never really delivered. And that gets him thinking about the shortness of life and the pointlessness of believing tomorrow is time enough. Growth is all around him. Even the graveyard is alive with primroses, splashing their old familiar brilliance against the leaden green of the long winter. The hardness of the roadside ditches is suddenly soft with unfolding buds. Life is going on, not just around the corner. The world is young again. He remembers a part of what living is all about.

Summer continues its procession. The notion of sex becomes a strange and twisted everything and nothing. When it's everything it's a release, a need, something essential to his survival, and when it's nothing it's a haunted absence, almost a sentence.

He checks the number. Again. He lifts the phone, dials, then puts it back in the cradle. Re-checks the number and dials again. He hears it ring. The evening sun catches the roof of the car. He prays for an answer. A cloud scuds across the face of the sun. He prays for no answer. Rain spots the window. The phone goes on ringing. The rain falls heavily on the garden. No one there. He tried, God knows he tried, it wasn't meant to be.

The attractions of liberty and independence pall every time he thinks about asking someone out. He thinks back to those early weeks when he expected to meet someone on the road or in the woods, someone as lost and in need of friendship and love as he was. And he thinks of the months in between when he descended into a limbo and lived without any positive passion.

Now that he has rediscovered his energy for intimacy, he feels like Robinson Crusoe, striding the boundaries of his island garden, uncertain as to his ability to manufacture a raft for escape. Uncertain, too, about whether he really wants to be out there on the seas at all. There's safety and a kind of comfort in being where he is —no possibilities, no opportunities for rejection.

He goes back to the comfort of making lists. He sits down and light-heartedly lists all the women he knows, anyone he'd feel comfortable asking out, women whose refusals could be couched and accepted with humour. The list runs to two people. It's a reminder of his isolation. He revisits every half-friendly greeting he can remember. The list lengthens. And then he thinks about the sadness of what he's doing. He's already trying to locate someone who will let him down gently if they're willing to pick him up in the first place. He's pretending at freedom, running from the risk and possibility of meeting someone new.

Just go out and do it, he tells himself.
Do what, go where, meet who?
There must be someone!
Must there? Why must there?
But there were all those possibilities.
Were. In your head.

He dreams of a beautiful young woman. She lives not far from the cottage. He meets her on the road, she cycling, he walking. She falls in love with him, love at first sight. She wants him so badly that she arrives late at night. It's pouring rain, she's soaked. He gives her a dressing gown. They sit in the firelight. She talks, he listens. She tells him how much she loves him, needs him. He wakes to a half-empty bed.

He starts the week, determined that by the weekend he'll at least have struck up a conversation with someone new and, perhaps, have asked them out. But the week is passing with only the promise of *next week*.

He tells himself he's still working things out with the children and that much is true. Their lives have reached a balance and he doesn't want to disturb that serenity. But that's only half the story, the rest is him. He wants love, he wants sex, he wants passion, he wants excitement but he wants them on his terms because he also wants freedom.

The few women friends he does have are kind to him and patient and loving. But he leans on them too much. He uses their friendship as a crutch and, in the end, the crutch splinters and breaks under the weight of his need or greed.

He is learning that friendship and love and kindness, no matter how deeply they run, can still run dry. He's learning that the best intentions in the world can not unravel damage that is absolute and low and hurtful. And he's learning the shocking depths of his own potential for self-pity.

In his pain, the pain he inflicts on some of those about him is irredeemable. And his greatest regret is the knowledge that he can never alter it. He will try but, already, he knows the wounds are too horrific to heal.

He's disgusted by his abuse of true friendship. He ignores good will that had its roots in his youth. He looks at the man he is and is surprised and frightened by his callousness. He dreads the thought of himself.

In the middle of all this, he reads the Bible, the Old Testament, the books he has never opened before. Ecclesiastes and Proverbs pour out their poetry.

What is twisted cannot be straightened, what is not there cannot be counted ... Much wisdom, much grief, the more knowledge the more sorrow ... In darkness arriving, in darkness departing, even his name is wrapped in darkness. Never seeing the sun, never knowing rest ... A man's conduct may strike him as pure; Yahweh, however, weighs the motives ... He who returns evil for good will not rid his house of evil.

If only he could learn from what he's reading! But he reads for beauty, not for wisdom or solace. He reads for love and loss and passion. He follows Isaac up the mountain. He watches Ruth from the headland of a field and falls in love with her.

Ruth said: 'Do not press me to leave you and to turn back from your company, for wherever you go, I will go, wherever you live, I will live. Your people shall be my people, and your God, my God. Wherever you die, I will die and there I will be buried. May Yahweh do this thing to me and more also, if even death should come between us.'

He listens to the passing cars on Saturday nights, coming back from the discotheque in the local hotel, each carrying another Ruth.

thirty

My brother owes me five bicycles. He's home for a week's holiday at the end of a summer working in Wall's ice-cream factory in London and we play football on the front lawn. He promises me a bicycle if I win. He persuades me to give him five goals up *because you're faster than I am*.

I am faster. I'm eleven years old and I can run for hours. There are disputes about goals, penalties that aren't given and late calls for time out.

'There's no time out in soccer,' I tell him.

'That's just my years of basketball breaking through,' he says, like he's been playing for the Harlem Globetrotters.

'Well I should have a free then.'

'All in good time.'

He wanders into the house and I sit on the ball, waiting. He doesn't reappear for fifteen minutes.

'Now where were we?'

'It's my free.'

'I don't think so.'

'Yes it is.'

'I really don't think so. Let's drop the ball.'

'It's my free.'

'That's not how I remember it.'

He grabs the back of my neck in an ass's bite and then quickly drops the ball and we play on. I win. I almost always win, even in the complicated, four-leg matches that he comes up with, matches that run over two days. Finally, he accepts defeat and promises to bring me a bike *the next time I'm down*.

And the next time, at Christmas, we take up where we left off and I win a seventh bike. By the time he completes his medical studies the bikes are a running joke and he owes me twelve.

The truth is that I don't care but I don't tell him so.

thirty-one

The potatoes are in flower and the peas arc twining their way along the trellis of tied sticks. There are blooms near the back-door step and the box hedge is neat where he clipped it. The garden looks as if it belongs with the cottage. It looks like it might yield sustenance.

He sets off walking the three miles to Castledermot. The evening is bright and warm. A few cars pass him on the road, otherwise he has the countryside to himself. Even the village is deserted and he can see, as soon as he reaches his father's gate that the car is not in the yard. So much for his unannounced visit!

Across the road, a football match is in progress, so he climbs the wall, walks through the thin line of trees he knew as *The Plantation* in childhood and stands on the sideline. Castledermot is playing a team from the north of the county. There are fifty or sixty people watching. He scans the crowd and nods at those he knows. Half-time comes and he thinks about leaving. He wants to go but feels he can't. If he goes his leaving will be noticed. He's a child again, wanting to do something but not having the courage to push through with it. There's no logic to his uncertainty, all he has to do is turn, walk through the belt of trees, climb the low wall and go but he doesn't. He's isolated. He wishes someone would talk to him. He wishes he could mingle in one of the knots of people near the goal, have a laugh, listen to the comments, throw in a few of his own, but that's impossible.

The match starts again, play see-saws from one end to the other. It's a closely fought game but he's not enjoying it. He smiles at the irony of it all. Everything has changed and nothing has changed. He's still the teacher or the teacher's son, still on the periphery. He still can't take that simple step and be one of the crowd.

Some hope, he thinks, of you asking someone out!

The ball sails over the bar and Castledermot are ahead. He follows the play, trying to lose himself in the game but he can only see himself as he imagines others see him, *a spare prick at a wedding*. That's how it feels.

Castledermot pulls two points clear, then three and then the final whistle blows an end to his misery. He waves to no one in particular and he's gone, through the trees, over the wall, striding like a power-walker out the Hallahoise road.

thirty-two

My father is passionate about football.

On Saturday nights, my mother finds a half-torn sheet from long ago and cuts it into a neat square. My father finds a thin, straight piece of stick in the shed. And I have my flag to wave on the sideline in Athy or Newbridge or Tullamore.

The Kildare team runs out of the dressing room, kicking the ball high into the air, where it seems to stay, held aloft by our cheers. That unbroken voice is mine.

Come on Kildare! Come on the Lily Whites!

And then there's the parade of heroes. And wearing number six is Mick Carolan, the greatest hero of them all.

One Sunday afternoon, sitting on the sideline in Athy, I'm eighteen inches from him as he stands back to kick a sideline ball. I wave my flag and he smiles at me and, reaching down, he tousles my hair. His white socks are pulled up knee-high and his lily-white shorts and jersey shimmer in the heat. It's as though God has parted the clouds and reached down from Heaven and touched me. And then he drives the ball over the bar and we rise as one and cheer his genius. And I wave my flag again.

Another half-torn sheet, a banner in the summer afternoon.

The Starlights are our neighbours and friends but they're our heroes, too. Our home-grown, end-of-the-road football idols. They came together in 1962 and they've been kicking together for three years now. They wear white jerseys, like the Kildare county team, but with a blue star on the breast and when we watch them we want to be them.

The seven Kelly brothers, from the Bungalow, are at the heart of the team. The Bungalow is where us kids gather to watch *Dragnet* on a Friday night. But, if Kelly's television, the only one on the road, keeps us entertained it isn't enough for the Kelly brothers. They're looking for real excitement and television isn't real. Excitement comes in the shape of a football team. Winning isn't what it's all about, getting out and playing is the thing.

Times are getting better in Castledermot, the same as everywhere. Even an eleven-year old knows this. When I was eight or nine there was little football and little food. One Monday morning fourteen young men caught the bus from the village, heading for England and work. But now the 1960s are here and my father reads Lemass's words about *the rising tide lifting all boats*. I see young men who went to jobs in London and Birmingham coming back to work at home. But there's little else for them in Castledermot, beyond the cinema and dances.

The way I hear it, every spring and summer evening a group of young men had gathered around the Brook – a stream that trickled into the river Lerr. They'd lie on the grass, talking, passing time. One evening, Jim Doyle of Ballyvass suggested they start a football team between them. In the following weeks, the plan was finalised and a group, mostly lads from Woodlands, formed a team. And so our heroes took the field and now we never miss a home match.

The Starlights are a ragged group – seven of the Kellys – PJ, Lar, Jim, Mick, Jack, Vincent and Kevin. Their cousins, Bob and Frank Gannon; Oliver and Michael Hennessy, Bill Hayden, Noel Leigh, Pat Keating, Mick and PJ Holloway, Bill Deverall, Bill Doran, Noel Leigh, Paddy Connell, Jimmy Byrne, Jimmy Loughman. And Pat Ward, a brilliant footballer who, as often as not, arrives without his boots. Mick Hickey will offer his, but they don't fit and Pat kicks them off and plays, to our delight, in two pairs of stockings.

The Starlights now have thirty players on the panel but, in the early weeks of their existence, they had the bare fifteen. Playing as Woodlands, a set of medals was put up and a match arranged against the regular Castledermot team. That was the legendary game of three referees. First with the whistle was our next-door neighbour, Jack Hickey, but a row started and he abandoned the job. Nicholas Wall took up next but he only lasted a quarter-of-an-hour. There was only one man left on the sideline who had the respect of all sides, Jack Connell, a local butcher. He got in and the game was played to a satisfactory conclusion. Or, at least, it was finished!

At the start of that year's championship the best of the two local teams was chosen to represent Castledermot in the county championship – among the first fifteen were three of the Woodlands players, Mick Kelly, Jim Kelly and Pat Ward.

Three minutes into that championship game, a player from Castledermot arrived late and Jim Kelly was called to the sideline to make way for him. His brother Mick, who was the goalkeeper, pulled off his jersey and wrapped it round the crossbar in disgust. It was clear when Pat Ward did likewise that if one Woodlands man wasn't good enough, then none was! And so the Starlights were born.

We know these stories like we know our catechism. We know the names and dates and scores of the matches the Starlights have played. We know it all and remember it all because it matters to us.

We *whippersnappers* collect the ball from behind the goal and hope, some day, to wear the Starlight jersey. We've never heard of a team with a real name before. All the teams we know take their names from towns or villages but the Starlights are different. No one is sure who decided on that name but it arrived. The choice of colour for the jerseys was obvious, pure white like the county, but some bright spark decided on the blue star. Mothers and sisters were drafted in to sew these on by hand.

The county heroes of the time are Mick Carolan and Kieran O'Malley and the Starlights set out to emulate them.

There are worrying days while they wait to see whether the County Board will affiliate the team. *Affiliation* is at the centre of every conversation on the road that week. Andy Hickey, one of the backroom team, talks about nothing else. He takes on the air of a man who knows something about these things, something no one else is privy to. He has an air of confidence about him.

I'm bloody well sure we'll be affiliated.

And they are!

Our heroes have hit the big time. New jerseys, new club, new name, it gives us Woodlands' and Abbeylands' kids a reason to be proud.

The team trains five nights a week, Monday to Friday, with a game on Sunday. On Thursday evenings, they gather round the outspread *The Nationalist*, to see who the weekend's opposition is. A Sunday without a game is like Doomsday.

For those who play, for those who watch, the games are not just a haze but rather a roll call of moves and saves and passes and fouls and scores.

There's the Sunday afternoon when Kevin Kelly hares up the wing and collects a ball around the half-way line, sees Pat Ward running up the other side and lofts the ball across to him. It lands straight in Pat's hands and he puts it over the bar. It all happens in one smooth and flowing move. A cheer goes up. It's something the team will talk about for weeks. It's something we'll try to copy day after day that long summer, the perfect move that might never be perfect again!

The Starlights play and lose and play and lose and play. But defeat never deters them and never makes us lose faith.

By now, the club is properly run, with committee, selectors, the lot. And the selectors don't simply go into a room: they go into *conclave*. It's a word we've learned from the recent election of the Pope. Players aren't allowed into these meetings under pain of being struck off the team. Everything is above board *without a hint of favouritism.*

The summer deepens and sometimes money is more plentiful. Sometimes, on a Saturday, one of the Starlights makes his way to Mac's in Carlow for a new pair of boots. Only the odd player can hope to buy a pair of Blackthorn boots, the ones with the low ankles. The best the rest can hope for are the bright, brown, cheap and heavy boots, with high ankles.

Away matches mean transport but transport is no great problem for the team because the Kelly's come to the rescue again. They're builders and they supply the transport in the form of a little green pick-up. The complete team, lock, stock and barrel, assemble on the back and away they go. We gather at the end of the road to watch them and wave them away, entirely optimistic that they'll bring home the bacon.

The truth is, defeat is almost certain. Nevertheless, the complete squad returns to Kelly's for tea and sandwiches. We kids, who never travel to away games, but never miss a home match or a training session, go down and knock on the door with the same question every Sunday evening: *Did yis win?* And the answer comes back: *Nearly.* Meanwhile, in the crowded kitchen the post-mortem continues. Post-mortems tend to last all week, till it's time for the next game.

Each Monday morning Kelly's wash-line dances to the tune of twenty-one jerseys. Week in, week out, they're all hand washed by Mrs Kelly and each player checks, as he passes the garden line, that his own number is safely there.

The Starlights stay together for four years. They play tournaments as far away as Tipperary – travelling in the pickup – and win one first-round championship match, against Kildangan, plus a couple of challenge games, but winning has little to do with the crack. The characters are numerous and even the legends become legendary.

One Sunday, to our amazement and delight, the three half-forwards on an opposing team bite the dust simultaneously. Another day, the full forward, Jack Fingleton, goes in heavily on a goalkeeper and is warned by the referee, Mick Leavy.

'You do that one more time, Jack, and to that line you're going,' he says.

Jack smiles, 'If I'm going, Mick, you're coming with me.'

Another Sunday, a double-header in Newbridge, the Starlights against Ballymore Eustace.

The Starlights are first out. It's a tough match. Afterwards, Kevin Kelly is going up onto the stand to watch the second game. A steward stops him for the two-bob admission fee. Kevin tells him he played in the first game.

'By God,' the steward says, 'you were a brave man.'

Differences of opinion, a polite way of describing tribal warfare, are part and parcel of the games and we live in hopes of seeing them, but even so they stay on the field. Once the game is over, done deeds are forgotten.

Fund-raising is a necessary part of keeping the Starlights on the field, and on the road. Flag-days are the bread and butter of the club. The players and selectors and hangers-on sit for hours on a Thursday night, in the room at the back of Kelly's shop, putting the pins in the flags, and come out with fingers bleeding. On the Saturday night they do the rounds in Carlow and Athy and Tullow, selling the flags in public houses. The following Tuesday night, after training, they count the proceeds. There's always someone who queries the take.

I thought we had a deal more nor that!

A suggestion for numbering the boxes is overruled. What you get is your lot.

But all of this is adult stuff, what we kids really want to see are the doings on the field. We want to see men like Frank Gannon who always, always wears his jersey over his working shirt.

It's pure, simple entertainment but it isn't just a game, it's a way of life. The players walk or cycle home in the falling night, talking about the training. We hear their laughter from the end of the road. Our mothers call us in but we hang back in the dusk, waiting to catch the last heroic words. And on Monday nights we listen while the previous day's game is analysed. There's no fancy gear and only one football. There's just a love of the game for its own sake.

And there are little victories, sweet moments against the odds.

PJ Kelly is sent off one night, early in a match, but, while the referee is down the other end of the field, he comes back in again. The Kellys all look alike and the referee had no idea who's who.

In 1965, I'm sent away to boarding school. My mother's letters keep me up to date on the team's progress through the winter leagues. She sends me match reports from *The Nationalist*. When I return for the summer holidays I pick up where I left off, following the Starlights.

For these summer nights and days theirs are the excitements I thrive on. The Starlights go from strength to strength, in spite of hard times.

Andy Hickey, the club treasurer, has a phrase when he makes up the accounts at the end of the year, *We're all square and I don't think that's bad at all*. It goes into Starlight history.

All the club meetings are held in the back room of Kelly's shop. They often last three or four hours and the business end is taken as seriously as the football, though the logic is sometimes surreal. At one meeting Joe "Rocks" Breslin proposes Billy Maher as trainer on the basis that *his legs are long enough to do the job.*

The wonder is that any meeting ever gets finished. Skidding our borrowed bikes in the sand outside, we can hear the *free-for-alls.*

But, even as youngsters, we see that there's something simple, something genuine about the Starlights and that very sincerity is part of what keeps the team spirit going.

One night, when Dan Byrne is training the team and they're on the end of a bad hammering and the edge is going out of the game, he calls Kevin Kelly to the sideline and whispers, urgently, *Start a row, start a row!*

Tactics vary, cloth is cut to measure.

In 1966 the new, young village Curate decides it's time to heal the local rift and reunite the teams. It's all over as quickly as it had begun, and by the end of that year the Starlights are no more. The white jerseys with the blue stars are collected, put in a bag and put away, forever. Someone has been overheard saying the Castledermot team will use the jerseys for practice matches. The Starlights decide otherwise.

They will not, ever.

The jerseys go out of circulation and remain out of circulation, legendary, like our own Shrouds of Turin.

And the players go their different ways. Football is no longer their life but, to us kids, they remain far more than a football team, they're our champions, everything we ever wanted to be.

thirty-three

The sun throws that particular light that says June. He's coming home from work. He turns the car into the lane beside the cottage and, for a split second, he sees a middle-aged man and a boy of nine or ten, standing on the step at the back door. He looks again, they're gone, just a shadow of the hedge thrown by the evening sun. He's not alarmed. He's pleased.

Getting out of the car, he stands at the end of the path. The swallows are genuflecting in and out of the open garage. He conjures the figures up again and follows them back to that other summer evening when his father and he called to this door, canvassing.

It's a spring evening in the early Sixties and they've left the Morris Minor up on the road and walked down the lane and in past the iron gates that hang from the granite pillars. The garden is neat and tidy, hollyhocks gaze inquisitively over the box hedging. An elderly lady, Julia Wilkie, comes to the door and greets his father warmly. She's dressed in a navy pinafore, the kind his grandmother wears, dotted with thousands of tiny red and white flowers. She calls a man's name and her brother, Tom, appears from the vegetable garden. The boy listens while they discuss the weather and the garden with his father.

He follows now, as the couple lead his father and the young boy between the neat, straight drills of cabbages and potatoes and onions and carrots. They stop to smell the rambling rose that climbs crazily across a trellis. They admire the way the sun is coming off the fields of young barley. Only after all of this, only after he has politely declined tea does his father proffer a handbill with his policies and his name on it.

'There's no need to ask,' the lady says. 'You'll be favoured with two votes here.'

And he believes her. There's a genuineness in her voice. Even as a small boy, he has come to recognise the true from the pretended promise.

He follows them back to the doorstep and gives his father and the young boy time to leave and the elderly couple time to fade.

Only then does he put his key in the lock and step inside.

As he eats his evening meal, he wonders what outstanding memories his children would choose from their times here. Something happy, he hopes. Something blessed with sunshine and long dry grass. Something echoing to the sound of feet running on dry earth and the sight of gnats gathering in the late evening light. Something viewed from outside, while moths are drawn through the wide-open windows by the solitary bulb burning in the still deserted house, something that smells of summer and laughter. Just as he would choose to remember days when his father's joy and his own were one, so he hopes his children will choose to remember days when pleasure was shared with him.

He thinks about his childhood and the children's. There are so few spaces where they're allowed the joy of boredom. He remembers getting up to all kinds of marvellous mischief out of boredom. He regrets that there can never be a question of the children setting off, as he did, at nine o'clock in the morning, across the fields, and returning at five or six that evening. There will never be a time when they and their friends will raid a potato field and build a campfire and roast potatoes under the stars.

Days as an altar boy in Castledermot. Himself and Joe Gannon and Paul Kane and Liam Mulhall fumbling into their surplices and soutanes, grabbing the candlesticks, the holy water and the thurible and rushing to be at the church door as a funeral arrives. Standing in the porch, the bell tolling slowly as the hearse noses its way into the churchyard. Watching as the coffin, its ornamentation telling nothing of a life, is carried inside. The shuffle of feet along the aisle, the smell of freshly cut timber, the priest's voice rising.

Dies irae, dies irem. Day of wrath, day of mourning. Out of the depths we cry to you, oh Lord. Lord hear our prayer.

And, afterwards, the Lord heard their laughter

Summer has settled on the fields and he knows it's going to be a good one. He wakes morning after morning, to blue skies and a smoky haze that drifts lazily away across the fields, unveiling, minute by minute, a shade of turquoise on the hills of Laois. Birds fly high, each an Icarus testing its wings against the heat of the sun.

June is about to slide into July and the potatoes are all in flower, British Queens and Home Guard. Day after day the old peony at the garage wall explodes blood red against the sun-washed wall. The swallows dive across the yard, delivering food to their young. In the evenings, when he gets in from work, the first thing he does is to open all the windows, freeing the heat from the house.

They're sitting in the garden at the table that's wobbling on the dry earth. They've been playing football and rounders and cricket and hide-and-seek. The last light is trickling from the hills. The school holidays are three days away. They haven't ventured inside all evening. They're eating by the light of the moon. The children are talking quietly.

'Wouldn't it be great if life was like this all the time?'

They take a picnic up Mullaghcreelan Hill, gather wild flowers along the roadside, watch for badgers and foxes, sit in the garden and wait for the first and second and third of the evening stars. They're happy.

So much of the summer still stretches before him and he's determined to enjoy it. He goes out, meets people, goes to plays and concerts.

The children have been away for a week and he has used the cottage as little more than a place to sleep. He's catching up with friends, having virtually disappeared for a year, surfacing as a solitary name on a Christmas card from a strange address. And now, here he is ringing or calling out of the blue.

He's making new acquaintances. Sometimes, as he leaves home to meet someone, he finds himself tempted back to carrying safety lists of things to talk about but he resists the temptation.

The summer is a good one, all in all. There are occasions that promise more than they deliver, there are confusions, mis-read situations, there's laughter – embarrassing and warm – but, above all, he's rediscovering the consolation of friendship.

But, every now and then, he feels a tap on the shoulder, something whispering that things are not quite right. He has to remind himself that he's all grown up, that he has to accept life the way it is and take responsibility for his own actions and feelings.

He's walking a hillside with a woman friend. They're talking about life and love and growing up. He's explaining himself to her, explaining why he can't commit himself, why he's unreliable. He's talking about childhood and the weight of responsibility.

'But you're not a child any more,' she says, sharply. 'You can't keep blaming *now* on *then*.'

She tells him some of the things she went through in her childhood. He listens in surprise. He has known her since teenage years but he never knew any of this.

'You have to get on, leave it behind. I've done it. I had to. You can't waste so much energy looking over your shoulder.'

But old habits die hard. Driving home that night he hears a voice accusing him: *you have no right to this, you'll pay for it, just mark my words.* Sometimes the voice is his own and sometimes it's his mother's and sometimes it's a chorus of those who he thinks despise him but it's never his father's voice: his father is never the one to question feelings.

At home, he lifts the phone and dials his friend's number but hangs up before she answers. A moment later the phone rings. He knows it's her. He lets the phone ring out.

Most of the time he keeps away from Castledermot and feels better for it. Out here, out in the country, he can be his own person. Among the people he grew up with he still feels uneasy. He buys his petrol in Castledermot, chats with Behans and visits his father. Otherwise, he avoids the village, apart from attending funerals.

His friend fumes down the phone, after he has cancelled a walk to go to a funeral. 'You're obsessed with funerals. You should have been an undertaker so you could mix business with pleasure, you already go to every funeral.'

The last part isn't true but the rest is reasonably accurate. There is, he has to admit, a strange tie that binds him to Castledermot. He is ill at ease there, yet he feels drawn to share its ritualistic moments of loss.

And he has to agree that there's something about the guise of death, the smell of incense and timber, the undeniable drama and emotion. But there's more to it than that, there's the communal sense of loss and survival and a need to be present.

thirty-four

In a corner of the garden, I've made my own graveyard.
Anything that dies, is buried there – pinkeens, butterflies,
wasps, bees, rabbits and The Little Green Man.

My father buried the rabbits there, without a proper
funeral, but that was because they'd been attacked and
blinded by the neighbours' chickens, while we were at an
auction, and they had to be put down quickly, out of their
misery. But all the rest get proper burials.

In summertime the funerals are mainly for pinkeens.
We catch them in the Brook and they live for a couple of
days in jam jars, on the windowsill outside the back door.
One pinkeen survived for three weeks and a day. That was
a record. But, in the end, every pinkeen turns white and
goes belly-up in the night.

This morning it's a Black Doctor, a big pinkeen with
a black belly. He's lying on his back, eyes wide open. The
water is dull. Two other pinkeens swim in circles. I get a
second jam jar and separate the dead one from the living
and lay it in an empty Calvita cheese box, lined with
grass.

I get a spade from the shed, go down the garden and dig a big hole. Only then do I call for Joe Whelan.

Joe is the undertaker and I'm the priest. I go inside and get an old scarf and put it round my neck as a stole. I fill a cup with water and pick a feather from the ground. I stand in the doorway of the shed. Joe carries the Calvita box from the shed and I sprinkle water on the coffin. Joe lays it on a small handcart we've tied to the back of the old tricycle. I say the prayers, picking bits of Latin from my memory of Mass.

Pater noster, ave Maria, benedictus, sanctus, nostris, panis angelicus, tantum ergo. Amen.

Then I deliver the sermon.

This man was a great man. He lived a good life. He leaves behind a wife and twenty children who have no money and no food. We pray for them now and forever and ever. Amen.

I walk around the coffin, sprinkling more water. That done, Joe sets off along the path, down between the apple trees, close to Hickey's fence, and across to the burial ground. The Calvita box bounces and rattles in the cart. I walk importantly behind, mumbling other bits and pieces of Latin.

At the graveside, I sprinkle more water. Then we stretch two pieces of twine across the open grave and lay the Calvita box on these. Slowly we lower the box into the ground, finely balanced on the twine. Next, we take two fireside shovels from the trailer and shovel the clay onto the cardboard box. There's something signifi-cant and final about that sound of the shovelled clay as it falls on the hollow box with the dried-out corpse inside.

Last of all, we make a cross with two sticks and a length of twine and put it above the grave, a cross like all the other crosses in that patch.

Sometimes, when pinkeens are scarce and bees are out of season, I bury The Little Green Man. He's a plastic man with a steering wheel in his hand, a man who came in a red racing car but the car is long lost. I bury him often but I always mark him well so that I can dig him up when real bodies are scarce.

When we move house in 1958, he travels with us. I bury him in the new garden, outside the sitting-room window, on the October day when Pope Pius XII is buried. My mother is listening to the funeral on the radio and I can hear it through the open window. For once, there's someone else to do the commentary and the Vatican choir is singing just for my Green Man. My mother laughs and says: *Now you're in your element.*

thirty-five

And yet there are days that contribute to the preservation of hope and optimism.

This July evening, he finds a woodbine plunging from the branches of a sycamore, deep in the woods of Mullaghcreelan. He brings home an armful of the flowers, drenching the house with their perfume. He'll walk Mullaghcreen Hill a hundred times afterwards, in other Julys, but already he knows he'll never find that particular woodbine again.

This evening, he sees a teenage couple kissing, near the water pump down the road. They're so rapt in each other that neither sees or hears him pass. Their bicycles lie against the ditch and there's a trickle of water on the dry clay beneath the pump where they bent to drink. He passes without resenting their happiness.

An August morning with mushrooms nudging the grass in the field at the foot of the hill and blackberries shining in the ditches as he walks home.

A late September night and candles burn in the sitting room, music and firelight and a feeling that is almost peace.

Clare, his novel, is published. The reviews are very positive. He begins work on a collection of stories. Whether the thought of the stories provides him with a form of exorcism, or whether familiarity is breeding some kind of content, he finds this second autumn in the cottage less depressing. The rain comes and the wind still sweeps up the fields from the Barrow valley but he gets on with his work. The cottage is more like home to him now.

He puts in bookshelves.

    'Dad, did you put up those shelves.'

    'Yeah. Do you like them?'

    'They're nice.'

    'Good.'

    A silence.

    'Dad?'

    'Yeah.'

    'Did you make them that way on purpose?'

    'How do you mean?'

    'Well, you know, slanted like that.'

    'You mean crooked?'

    'Ah … yeah.'

He has his books. He has his CDs. He seldom watches television.

    The leaves turn, the storms blow the leaves away, there's frost, settling lightly on the roof, coating the sheltering straw that's twisted round the water pump. He stacks firewood in the garage and dries it beside the range. The sunflowers spill their seed back into the garden. He burns orange peels in the dying fire and the smell reminds him of another, more distant, past, of another part of childhood.

The swallows are long gone and he has put away the wooden garden seat the children made. The last of the dahlias have bowed their heads and dropped their petals onto the misty clay. Even the long yellow grasses near the wire fence at the garden's end are shrinking back into the ground. The sycamores in Mullaghcreelan Wood have turned and every breeze throws a fresh spread of leaves over the roadway. Walking in the forest on windy days has become a game of tig as the chestnuts drop in handfuls from the trees above the path.

Another relationship has petered out and no amount of pretending or sex can disguise that fact. He's left with the memory of physical comfort. Loneliness is at his shoulder again, creeping up quietly, persistently.

An October evening and he's thinking about an old friend he hasn't seen or spoken to in ages. The bits and pieces of a love affair fall back into place. He thinks about another October, almost twenty years ago, when he went to visit her at her parents' home. He remembers the smell of old books and spent ash in the fireplace. He remembers afternoons walking on the hills with her, dusk falling on an empty beach, lying in long dry grass, the sky blue above them, the memory of clover, red and white, beneath their heads.

And he thinks of winter days in Dublin, cycling home from college, stopping to pick up groceries, lighting a fire in the big, empty fireplace. Making soup, listening to the couple upstairs making love, laughing with friends. Walking through the college grounds, dodging the sudden, bitter November showers. Sitting at the front window of the flat in Rathmines as snow fell, dreaming about the maybes and the mights of their lives.

He thinks of a December weekend when she came to stay at his parents' house. He remembers a frost-filled winter night. They were driving home from a dance in Carlow and he'd parked the car in a gateway near Prumplestown Crossroads, off the main road. He remembers her body beautiful across the front seats of the car, her head on his lap, the full moonlight whitening her skin. The radio was playing but they turned it off and listened to the quietness outside until the windows frosted over and she pulled on her jumper and smiled at him.

He remembers another night, the same weekend or another one that winter, in the kitchen. His parents were asleep upstairs and they'd come back from a midnight walk and taken off their coats and then the rest of their clothes and stood against the kitchen door, kissing, their bodies close, making love but not fucking, not speaking, listening for a footstep on the stairs. Listening, breathing quietly, holding each other, not wanting to go to their separate beds.

He longs for days like that again, for the excitement and the comfort that were there in equal measure. He finds the woman's phone number. He thinks about ringing her but in the end he doesn't because …

Because, what is there to say? *Hello, this is me. How are things with you? I just decided to give you a call.* That kind of pointless small talk.

Because, in some kind of mad rush of blood to the heart, he might tell her the truth, that he's been thinking of the night in the car and the moon on her body and his lips on her breast. And what then? Silence, an embarrassed giggle, a quick and awkward change of subject, the sound of a phone being hung up?

Because, she'll have her own memories or, perhaps, there's nothing worth her while remembering. Perhaps this is all him.

Because, because, because ...

Whatever the fascination, those memories have walked him past his forty-first birthday and out of October, not stumbling in some awkward mid-life crisis but gently, because they've brought no regrets, no sense of a necessary penitence.

thirty-six

It's September, the week before I go back to boarding school, and the sun is coming up and I whistle the dogs, Brandy and Soda, out of their shed and we cut across the football field, through Dempsey's fields, over Joe Shea's bridge and up the side of Rice's Hill in search of mushrooms.

The sheepdogs scurry and nose along the banks of the Lerr. I climb the gate from one field into another, and immediately the grass is salted with button mushrooms. I pick and thread them on hanks of thin, strong grass. The dogs come running, checking on me, and then they are gone again. Rabbits watch, unperturbed, from the long shadows of the brambles. Each time I lace a stalk of grass through mushroom flesh, I smell the biting, earthy smell that's almost taste.

There are more mushrooms here than I'll ever need so I finish my picking and leave five hanks in the grass near a rock and walk on up the sloping field and into the shelter of the furze bushes that were a childhood playground. In there we could take off our clothes and paint our bodies with the juices of fruit or the green of dock leaves and play at Indians. We had hideouts and booby-trapped pathways and meeting places that the gangs from the other end of the village would never find. There were warrens of passageways through the thorny undergrowth and only we knew where they led.

But on this honeyed morning Rice's Hill looks down over a village touched by frost, dressed in a flimsy haze. From up here, the ruined abbey dominates the skyline. I remember nights as a child, walking to October devotions in the church, seeing Rice's Hill ablaze as the gorse was burned. But, always, the grasses clawed back and the furze took hold again.

Below me, the Little Hill protects the sleeping silver river in the long shadow of morning. And then, as I watch, the rising sunlight drops into the water and it comes alive again. The broken stones, where the river Lerr and the Brook converge, catch fire as the granite kindles in the new light. For an instant, I'm raking the ashes of a long forgotten afternoon campfire and then the sun sweeps like a bright cloud across the hillside and the morning is warm.

I walk up to the Big Rock and remember how we lay there naked and guileless in the sun, young Indian braves roaming the Arizona wilderness, planning our attacks on wagon trains beyond the sloes.

The dogs follow me to the Little Hollow where we finalised our plans for warfare. This is the same hollow where, as boys of eleven and twelve, we played cards and imagined girls. This is the same hollow where now, as teenagers, uncertain seed is spilled.

The sun is fully up now, wringing the frost and dew from autumn trees. I walk back down the field, collect the mushrooms, whistle the dogs from the undergrowth and turn for home.

thirty-seven

He sits in the restaurant and orders lunch. Opening the paper, he turns to the sports page. He's lost in some story when there's a voice at his shoulder.

'Are you waiting for someone?'

His wife is standing beside the table.

'No, no, are you?'

'No, I just dropped in to have a sandwich.'

'You're welcome to join me, if you'd like.'

'You're sure?'

'Yes. Of course.'

He folds the paper and they sit across the table from each other. The waitress takes their orders. Music is playing in the background.

'Well, how's country life?'

'Not bad, OK.'

'Good.'

'And you? How's school? Are you glad to be back?'

She laughs.

'It's like that?'

'Same old, same old.'

He nods.

The music rolls in, filling the beached silence. The waitress brings their food. They eat. It's easier than talking.

'The kids seem to be in good form.'

'Great. They're looking forward to Christmas already.'

'Do they know what they'd like Santa to bring them?'

'Lots of things but they haven't finally decided.'

'Right.'

'I'll get them to write their letters in the next few weeks. Give him plenty of time.'

'Good.'

'So, are you doing anything exciting?'

'Not really, working on the book.'

'Right.'

'I'm trying to make things better – when they're out with me. We're having fewer rows.'

'That's good.'

'Do they say anything?'

'Not a lot but I think they're more settled.'

'Do you really think so?'

'I do.'

The coffee arrives and the music goes on.

'And how are you?'

'I'm fine,' she says.

'Are you?'

'Yes, I am.'

'Would you tell me if you weren't?'

She smiles a dark smile.

'Would there be any point?'

thirty-eight

The bell goes, the Brother closes his book, bags clatter off the floor and copies are crammed in. One boy pulls the remnants of his lunch from the bottom of his satchel, chewing on a jam sandwich that might be a piece of amputated flesh. The door is open, the sun is coming in off the concrete yard and we're rushing, crushing, to embrace it.

'Take it easy, lads,' the Brother says. 'It'll wait for you.'

The sunlight is falling between the golden leaves of the tremendous chestnut that umbrellas the playground. We pour into its honeyed shades, into the late October warmth, into the fresh and laughing day that still has life in it, this day that has waited for us like a patient dog.

We're free. Racing down the yard, through flung-open gates, onto St John's Lane and down past the Brothers' house. Away, away from confinement to everything that promises a weekend of conkers, football, running, anything.

thirty-nine

He looks between the parted curtains at the rain sweeping down over the trees and into the saturated front garden. He stumbles out of bed and feels the seeping dampness on the wall beneath the window.

In the kitchen he plugs in the kettle. The fields, below the garden, are green but it's a damp, dark, green. The kettle steams and the rain lifts and clatters like a bead curtain against the window.

He goes and stands under the hot shower and tries to imagine summer and open windows and sunlight already warm on the empty chairs.

And then he goes back to the kitchen, rubbing a hole in the steam on the window, sipping tea, peeping out at a day that he knows will not improve. He thinks about the story he's working on, the hole it's in. He think about the jobs he's had over the years – builder's labourer, permanent-way maintenance man on the railway, gardener, kitchen porter, washer-up. Better a writer on a morning like this.

The rain is coming straight down the sitting room chimney, pitting and pocking the dead ashes from the night before.

At least there's a load of dry sticks in the garage. He won't have to go stick collecting till the afternoon. By then the rain may have eased.

All the cottages along the side of the valley are hunched against the incoming rain and wind and sleet and snow. And all are open, in turn, to the afternoon and evening sun. He loves that fact. Not the cold and wind for themselves but the fact of living in the face of the weather. He's always loved the elemental, the rawness of weather.

As a child, there was nothing he loved more than pulling on his coat and boots and getting out in the rain. He loved the rough edge to the day, the barber sharpness of the wind, the way rain would soak the ends of his jumper sleeves or how sleet insinuated itself down the back of his coat collar, slipping cold and wet inside his shirt.

In his teenage winters, he loved walking fields of snow, setting off well-wrapped up, making the first crunched boot marks in the emptiness. Climbing fences where the snow fell again as he put his hand on the barbed wire, following the flow of the black Lerr through the bleached and frosted landscape. And later the wind chilled and burned and the snow worked its way inside his boots and the hardening frost and the falling night made the going harder, but that was part of the challenge, part of the discomfort, part of the pleasure. There was something about being on that edge of difficulty that was exhilarating.

The only place to meet weather is face to face, on its own terms, in its own setting. In a small boat on a morning river, in the night when the mist is thicker than the darkness, naked in a cornfield in August, in February when the puddled ice is sharper than broken glass. When summer breathes its lilac breath from ditches. When the rain is like a graveside. Those are the times when there's no escaping what weather is about, no escaping the rudiments of the air and the countryside. Out there the weather is different, out there it isn't just an inconvenience between high buildings.

He loves weather, whatever it offers, and the more extreme the offering the better.

forty

A dark afternoon in the middle of a week in the middle of a winter, and it's raining and I see Tom Forrestal coming slowly up the Low Terrace, leading his huge white horse by the headband, the dust cart rumbling and jumping on its wooden wheels behind them. The rain is tilting down, between empty trees long abandoned by the birds, forking into his face. The horse stops at Whelan's gate and I kneel up on my chair at Mammy K's kitchen window and pull back the corner of the curtain.

Tom Forrestal hoists a dustbin onto his shoulder and heels it over the high side of the enormous cart. He lifts it like I've seen my father lift a sack of seed potatoes, lightly, easily, without even noticing the weight. The dreary afternoon is shaking out the last of its light and Tom is shaking out the last of the rubbish from Howe's bin, and I can see the rain running down the horse's face. Now he comes to Mammy K's gate and the bin is in his arms, then on his shoulder, like a ballerina, before her unpinned hair, the waste of another week, tumbles onto the wooden floor of the cart. And then he puts the bin gently back on the wet grass at the gate and looks up and waves and smiles and I wave back and I see the rain dripping off the sack that hoods his head. It falls onto his face and steam is rising off the horse's flanks. And I hear the dull rumble of the cart wheels on the road and I wish I was out there because the rain and the heavy bins and the dripping hood and the soaking coat never wipe the smile from this man's face. I want to be out there with the horse. I want to do Tom's job, to be out where I can't be.

It's spring now and Joe Whelan and myself are sitting on the ditch between Whelan's and Behan's. Tom Forrestal is tacking the big white mare and the single plough is lined up and speared into the earth and he *hups* the mare and then she moves slowly, her heavy feet rising lightly and stepping the length of the garden. At the other end, he turns the mare and plough and she plods back up the incline, her head high, the plough glinting in the evening sun.

Tom's eyes are on the furrow.

All evening, they go up and down the long garden: horse and plough and man. And all evening Joe and I sit on the ditch watching, silent. Finally, when the last furrow is turned and the plough is left on the headland, Tom Forrestal looks up and nods. We slide down the side of the bank and he hoists us up and our legs grow short against the breadth of the mare's back. And he leads the animal down the garden and back up and we hold on for dear life. And then he lifts us onto the cloddy earth, and we scramble up the bank and watch as man and beast move out by the side of Behan's house. Only then do we speak and our words come out in whispers.

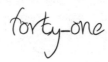

forty-one

The phone rings. It's his sister, checking that he's alive, checking that he's surviving. It's his brother, offering support.

He appreciates their concern. It's good to hear their voices. They chat about their lives and what they're doing, the usual chit-chat of brothers and sisters. He knows they want to reassure him and be reassured that he's managing. Their interest isn't in the nitty-gritty details of his life, there's never any element of prying into that; it's simply family concern.

Yet, he finds it impossible to be honest and open about exactly how he is coping. He passes on the local news, tells them who has died and who said what and how he's faring with work and writing. But he never really opens himself to them, he can't.

He realises, probably for the first time, that brother-hood and sisterhood mean more than the mere accident of birth. He recognises the difference between concern and love. He feels a real gratitude for the support he's getting. And yet he can't open his heart about the things that matter or bleed or scar him.

What he does see, through all of this, is the extraordinary closeness between his own children. They fight, of course they do, but there's a unity that he envies and delights in.

His daughter insisting that her toddler brother had to totter out to see his first remembered snow which, she told him, was *deep as a goose*.

And when, as small children, they planned to run away because they hadn't been allowed to stay up late, they did so together. Packing their books and teddy bears in one bag and standing side by side in the front porch, deciding it might be better to wait until the morrow, until the sun appeared.

He might be a *pest* and she might be a *pain* but he's her pest and she's his pain. They have that bond and he hopes they never lose it, that binding tie that will never grow awkward, that nothing can destroy.

forty-two

It's a wet, Wednesday afternoon and school is over. I troop reluctantly down to the YMCA hall on the Main Street. It's a place that's out of bounds to us kids at all other times, but on Wednesdays we shuffle in off the cold, wet path and dump our school bags in a corner and drag the wooden chairs with the heavy metal legs from the awkward, rickety stack in the corner.

The stove is lighting and I think about sitting near it. If I do, my clothes will dry more quickly and I'll have the comfort of its heat on my bare legs. The drawback is that I'll be in the front row when it comes to being asked to perform.

My mother thinks it's good for me to play a musical instrument. My brother and sister play piano but I have no musical gift. On Saturdays I go down to the convent and pick through tunes and play scales and come out with my knuckles red and singing from the constant raps of Sister Augustine's pencil. And on Wednesdays, like today, I come to the YMCA for harmonica classes. I don't even know the teacher's name. He's a sad and tired-looking man in a shabby overcoat who arrives in a small car *from Dublin or somewhere* and comes in, week after week, carrying a case of harmonicas.

Mouth oregons to us.

We're each supposed to have our own instrument. Each originally came wrapped in tissue paper inside a small cardboard box. Each was gleaming then, the mouth holes clean and dry. Now we pull them from pockets or hunt them out of the bottoms of schoolbags. Most of us have lost the boxes and the chrome backs, when they appear, are dull and discoloured, the mouthpieces clogged with spit and bits of dried sweets. And always, week in, week out, a quarter of the class arrives without its instruments.

I choose a seat in the second row, to the side of the stove, warm but not front line. The hands go up, the litany begins.

'Sorry, sir, me mother forgot to put me mouth oregon in me bag.'

'Sorry, sir, I was practising the whole week and I forgot to put it back.'

We snigger, having heard that one before.

'I have the box, sir, look, but the mouth oregon isn't in it, me brother must've took it out.'

The teacher patiently opens his case and doles out the loans. Taking these instruments, we examine them for spit but, as ever, they're clean.

'Right,' the teacher says, 'everybody ready?'

'Yes, sir.'

'Sir, can I go to the toilet?'

'Hurry on. The rest of us will start with "The Red River Valley." Key of G. And one, two, three …'

A sound comes out, a sweet sound that says *Come and sit by my side if you love me, do not hasten to bid me adieu.*

And then it's drowned by other sounds as we overpower the teacher's playing and saw our way to the end.

'Not bad at all,' he says.

He always says that.

'Now, once again, and watch my hand for the rhythm. *Remember* the *Red* River *Valley* and the *boy* that has *loved* you so *true.*'

I watch his hand and miss the notes. All I can hear is the whine of my own harmonica drowning the rest. We finish and he smiles.

'Not bad, not bad,' he says again. 'Now we'll have a solo. Who will it be?'

He looks along the rows of boys and girls. His eyes meet mine. I smile a petrified smile. He passes on. I relax.

'Ann, will you play something for us?'

'Yes, sir.'

'How about "Auld Lang Syne".'

'Yes, sir.'

The girl coughs and clears her throat and her face is red, but when she puts her lips to the mouthpiece the notes come out, slow and true. The teacher smiles.

'Good girl, well done. You could all do that, everyone of you could play that well, it's all a matter of practising.'

I don't know if he believes what he's saying but I know I don't. I'll never play that well or anything like it. I'll never get beyond the scales, just as I'll never get past a hacked-out version of the Preliminary Grade piano exam pieces.

'Right,' he says and he's still smiling. He doesn't look as tired as he did when he arrived. 'One more solo. Paddy?'

A boy on the other side of the room foosters with his sheet music.

We listen to an approximation of "Home on the Range" and then we all play it together and then we do our scales and the other pieces we're learning and then the class is over. The teacher gathers the loaned mouth organs and collects our six-penny pieces and closes his case and says goodbye. He's driving on to Carlow to another class and, after that, he'll go to Tullow and some other small and scattered towns.

We drag the chairs back to the corners and carefully arrange them in such a way that the whole collection will fall the next time someone touches them. Only then does the boy who went to the toilet reappear. He's been in there for forty minutes, forgotten.

'Thanks be to Jasus that's over, I never looked at th'oregon the whole week,' he says and he's laughing. 'And I got to keep me six-pence.'

Outside, it's still raining and the night is coming down and I pull my bag onto my shoulder and head for home. I hope the car will be in the yard when I get to the house. I hope my father will be home. If he's not in by now it could be all hours; he's been late the last two nights, long after I've gone to bed.

The gate is closed and the garage is empty. My mother and I sit down to our tea together.

It used to be Friday night was music night, she says sharply, *it seems to be every night this week.*

Later, I lie awake, listening, watching car lights slide along the electric wires, waiting for the recognisable engine sound, waiting for each car to slow at our gate. I fall asleep and wake and fall asleep again. Much later, I waken to the sound of angry voices in the kitchen. I creep down the stairs and sit on the fifth last step, where the wall ends and the banisters begin. The row goes on, the same row that has continued, on and off, over weeks and months and years. It's a row I've been listening to all my life, littered with the same words and phrases. I hear them now, *a drink or two ... all hours ... needs freedom ... call that freedom ... some bit of independence ... where does the money come from ... have to have some enjoyment ... a sense of responsibility ... bloody nagging ... oh yes always the big fellow ... I should have listened ... well, so should I.*

I hear my name used as ammunition and then the rigmarole starts again and finally, at last, there's silence and I hear footsteps and I hare back up the stairs and burrow under my bedclothes, holding my breath. There's the creaking of the second and third boards on the landing, someone in the bathroom. My father's footsteps in my room, that heavy smell of beer, the sound of his clothes laid across the back of a chair. I keep my eyes shut tight until I hear him getting into my brother's empty single bed. And then there's his sleeping breath and peace and I relax.

forty-three

And, now that the autumn is dripping into winter, he begins to work seriously on the stories for the book that will become *A year of our lives*. And he goes back to Leonard Cohen.

The deceptive simplicity of the melodies and the depth of the lyrics have long been his succour.

He first heard Cohen in the summer of 1971. That June, he finished his first year in college and started work as a builder's labourer.

It was a summer generous with promise. He was eighteen. He was going out with a beautiful girl he'd met the previous Christmas. He'd passed his exams. The weather was fine, he'd just got his driving licence and had money in his pocket.

On his second Friday in work he collected his pay packet, came home, had his dinner and showered. He was feeling a bit under the weather but put it down to the sun. He'd arranged to meet his girlfriend and go to the pictures.

By the time he'd driven the seventeen miles to her house, he felt worse. She suggested they go for a walk.

The evening was glorious. The sky was blue and taut, a yellow sun still hanging hot above the cornfields. They sat on an abandoned roller and he shaded his eyes from the light. She asked if he was all right. He told her he had a headache and that his eyes were sore.

'You should get home,' she said.

'I'll be OK.'

'You don't look OK. I want you to get home.'

He didn't argue.

Driving back, cars swam in and out of sight. He took an old pair of sunglasses from the glove compartment and put them on but they didn't help. His head was drumming and his sight was blurring. He stopped the car and got out. Kneeling on the roadside, he vomited. He believed he was going to die but he wanted to get home before he did. He had to get home, he didn't want to die so far from his family. He drove slowly, stopping when he needed to.

He had no recollection of parking the car and the next ten days became a mist of voices. Dr Dyer in the middle of the night, injecting him, whispering something about it not being safe to move him. The local priest in the morning, anointing him. He recognised the words, the Last Rites. He wanted to die, he was happy at the thought of an end to this withering, burning pain. Whatever was out there, something or nothing, it had to be better than this. His parents came and went almost silently, replacing the wet towels on his eyes and head. His father blacked out the bedroom window. The doctor called again, another injection and, in between, the constant, searing pain in his head and eyes. And then he woke and something had changed. The pain was still there but it was bearable. He heard his parents talking and their voices were lighter. The priest called again but now he joked with him about doing anything to get out of work. The doctor was smiling as he explained about meningitis. John could see again, the pale glow of the summer sun stitching through the blackout curtain his father had hung in the window.

His parents came and sat on the side of his bed.

His mother said, 'We thought we were going to lose you, it was touch-and-go.'

'It's hard to kill a bad thing,' his father laughed.

He saw relief in their eyes.

His sister brought the record player up from the sitting room. Margaret Behan sent over some records, among them *Songs From a Room* by Leonard Cohen. He'd never heard of him but immediately fell in love with his music. From the quiet opening lines of *Like a bird on the wire, like a drunk in a midnight choir, I have tried in my way to be free* he was engrossed. It had nothing to do with brushing death, it had to do with the beauty of word and voice and melody.

And when *Nancy wore green stockings and slept with everyone*, he wanted to sleep with his girlfriend. He just wanted her to be there with him, to kiss him and hold him and know that life was good. He wanted her to know how much he loved her.

He lay in bed and lusted after her. He knew she'd phoned everyday while he was sick, and still phoned but his mother wouldn't let him out of bed to talk to her. So when Leonard Cohen sang *I cannot follow you my love, you cannot follow me* he was singing for them.

Two weeks later, when he was well enough to go out, he bought a guitar which, like the piano and the harmonica, he never mastered. He also bought *Songs From a Room* and *Songs of Leonard Cohen* and taped them for his girlfriend and she fell in love with them, too.

And, in September, she fell in love with a young guy with sunburnt skin and dark good looks, a Canadian like Cohen. John sat across a campfire from them and listened while the Canadian played guitar and sang songs and, later, he watched them kiss. And he drove the same road he had driven blindly in June, only this time he was blinded by tears.

He remembers this and thinks about the loss of love and how loss cuts deeper and pain gets harder to heal. And, sometimes, when he thinks about the summer gone by, it reminds him of that strange, inspiring lost summer more than twenty years before. And he thinks about illness and being alone with it and he blesses the fact that he hasn't been physically ill at all since moving to the cottage.

forty-four

It's a dusty, dusky summer evening and we're coming home the long way from Mullarney, dragging ourselves through the sorrel fields, up the hill and out at the Cuckoo steps and then onto the Fraughan Hill road. There are five or six of us, and our sandalled feet are brown from the sunshine and dry clay of another sunny day.

And then we come to the gate of Joe Clinton's overgrown, rusted farmyard and dare each other to go in but none of us will.

'Are you mad? He's a crazy man, he comes down the lane sometimes and tries to kill people. He has loads of bodies buried in the yard. No one ever went in there and came out again.'

'So why don't the guards put him in jail?'

'They can't find the bodies, he boils them and burns them and ates the remainder. He lives up there because he hates people.'

Sometimes we see him in the street, driving his battered car or collecting his newspaper from Abbot's. And, when his name comes up at home – he's on the same committees as my parents – I keep my mouth shut. Anyway, I'm not supposed to be up on Crop Hill.

And even when we meet him in the shops or on the street, we never speak. None of us dares do that. We think of him as some kind of hermit whose door is never darkened by any living soul other than himself. We imagine him as a dark shadow, among the other shadows in the yard at the top of the lane.

Years after our childhood excursions, as a young history teacher in the local school, I contact Joe Clinton about his collection of memorabilia. He still lives on his hill farm, on the side of Crop Hill, but his interest in farming is fired only by his need to survive. His passion is history. Some people say he studied for the priesthood and that's where his interest in reading and history and education began. He's a thin man, dressed forever in shabby clothes, the arms of his sports jacket mended with leather patches. His elderly car runs down into the village and then chutters slowly back up again.

He invites me up to the farm. It's a warm, May evening but, even so, the creak of the farm gate stirs old childhood memories. The farmyard itself turns out to be a wonderful spot, sheltered by the farmhouse and the outhouses, overgrown and littered with the reminders of a life spent farming by a man who had no interest in farm work. The abandoned machinery is rusted and chained to the earth by thick weeds and dogged nettles

Inside, the house is a dusty confusion. There are publications everywhere — historical journals, newspapers, magazines, hardbacks, paperbacks, cuttings, photographs. The past spills from chairs and hides under tables, tumbles from presses and hangs valiantly onto bookshelves. And the small space between these and the artefacts he's collected over the years is where Joe Clinton lives. That limited infinity where he enjoys his life and breathes and soaks up the things that consume him, the stories and histories on which he thrived while his fields became a wilderness.

He takes down his good cups and saucers and plates and dusts them. He wets the tea and cuts fruitcake. He makes a space on a corner of the kitchen table, pushing back the books and papers, and we sit and talk and drink two pots of tea. And every couple of minutes he's up and down, searching out another book, spreading a map across the table, enthusing about something or other that he stumbled on in the course of his research.

And, while we talk, the light changes, the way it does unnoticed when you're lost in conversation, ebbing away through the moth-eaten curtains and dodging across the yard, retreating behind the rusting tractor parts and the plough that lies forever stranded, far from the fields it once turned.

And I watch the dim figure across the table and listen to his endless stories and theories and I think of the gaggle of children, gathered all those years ago at the gate of the lane. And I want to tell him how sorry I am for the way we took his good name.

'We used to come to your gate, as children. We never had the courage to come up here. We thought the place was haunted.'

He laughs a quiet laugh.

'I'm not surprised. Some nights, when it's dark and wet and windy, I'm not too pushed about coming home here myself.'

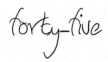

forty-five

His daughter has started in secondary school. She's still only twelve but, suddenly, his mind is focused on teenage. The biggest problem in being the parent of teenagers, John reckons, is the fact that you know the pitfalls because you had to go through adolescence to get to parenthood.

They'd had a relatively good summer. There have been rows but nothing out of the ordinary and nothing he hasn't managed to handle reasonably well. But just when he thinks of congratulating himself, his own head seems to find a hundred reasons to be hopeless. It isn't simply the onset of winter – though that doesn't help – but the wall of responsibilities that suddenly rises in front of him. His father is ill. His wife and he are reaching a stage where they need to tell the children they won't be living together again. He knows Hallahoise Cottage isn't going to be available forever, so he needs to start looking for a new house. And his friend, Jo Walsh, has died.

He met Jo in July when he set out to make a series of radio programmes with someone who was dying. Through the Hospice he made contact with this vibrant, warm, young woman in her early thirties. A mother of three, she lived less than twenty miles from him and, from the first day they met, they got on like a house on fire.

One afternoon they drove to her parents' house in south County Carlow and walked the banks of the canal. She chatted about her childhood and her own young family and her husband. She laughed and cried and cursed her cancer.

They watched the boats going up and down the water. They walked through her parents' garden. She advised him about his life and children and happiness.

As the summer wore on, she came to the radio station and he visited her at home and made some more recordings. Slowly, her bones broke down and she could no longer drive or walk. Sometimes they talked for hours without ever turning on the tape recorder.

She'd ring him at home, out of the blue, and they'd talk about how she was feeling, how his life was going, about her children and his, about anything and nothing. That was the joy of the friendship, there were no dues to be paid, on either side.

In early autumn, Jo moved back to her parents' house. He went to see her one afternoon but left the tape recorder in the boot of the car. It wasn't a time for recording, it was a time for goodbyes.

The rain is sheeting down. He walks with the throng and watches while her coffin is lowered. It's a cold, dark, bitter afternoon.

Her death hits him hard because he believed in her. He firmly believed she'd live to see her daughter's First Communion. He believed her when she laughed in the face of pain.

Her death depresses him because there's no logic to it. She was a beautiful woman, she adored her children, she was happy for them, she wanted so much for them and she was determined to be there with them. And it depresses him because he fell in love with her strength and her humour and her courage. In spite of everything, she was open to laughter and friendship and life but that wasn't enough.

At home, he's short tempered again, dismissive, reclusive. Much of the good he's done over the summer is beginning to unravel, but he determines not to let that happen. He fears for the children. He fears for the love they have for him. In spite of everything, their love remains. It deserves a greater respect than he's given it.

So he makes another effort. It's a huge undertaking because the black clouds are coming down. Most days, he wakes in a state of panic at the thought of the things he has to do, at the thought of his father's illness, at the thought of death, often at the thought of life. And once depression has its foot in the door, it refuses to leave. But at least, this winter, he keeps it locked, for the most part, in one room. Still, when it escapes, it comes out black and laughing.

He meets his wife. They talk about the situation. They accept that things are not going to change, there's no grand reconciliation on the horizon. They discuss how best to tell the children. It seems the time is as right as it ever will be.

This weekend.

This weekend they sit down with the children. They're two bundles of nerves, shaking and tense. They've worked out how the news should be broken. They agree that it's important to do it right, with the correct degree of *gravitas* but without making too great an issue of it. After all, they've been living in separate houses now for well over a year, but they recognise that it's one thing to live apart, one thing to come to self-recognition, one thing to accept facts about each other – but this is something else altogether. This is putting a final imprimatur on their situation. So, they tell the children how much they love them. They reassure them that they love each other. They explain how they've decided not to live together anymore.

The children look at them in amazement.

John feels sweat on his forehead.

'But we knew that,' his daughter says. 'We're not stupid. We knew that a long time ago.'

forty-six

It's a wet Saturday afternoon. My father comes into the kitchen.

'We're going to Athy,' he says.

'Can I stay here?'

I spend Monday to Friday at school in Athy. I don't want to spend a wet Saturday there as well.

'I'd like you to come with us. There's something I want you to see.'

'What?'

'Just something.'

'I think you should come,' my mother adds.

I'm intrigued. This isn't like them at all. Normally, they're happy for me to stay at home while they go shopping.

After we drop my mother at the Square in Athy my father drives to the railway station. We get out of the Morris Minor, pulling on our raincoats, and walk up to the signal-cabin, my father's workplace. Joe Murphy is sitting at the fire, smoke drifting from the damp turf.

'Is she on,' my father asks?

'A couple of minutes. She cleared Kildare a while back.'

I follow my father back down the slippery cabin steps, past the water tower and up onto the platform. We stand in the shelter of the waiting room and then I hear a train and my father steps outside. I follow him. A black steam engine hoots beneath the Town Bridge, the arch damping the smoke and pushing it back onto the open cab.

The brakes scream out along the wet rails and the train comes to a halt. I follow my father down the platform. The engine driver leans over the side of the cab and greets us.

'A bad day for it,' my father says.

'Rotten,' the driver nods.

'Would you mind if we took a spin with you, out to the bridge?'

'Not at all, hop up.'

I'm lifted high in the air, up onto the metal running plate and I move between the driver and the stoker, in the hot, open cab. Rain spits off the boiler. My father climbs up after me. The signal changes, the huge engine grinds slowly down the line, past the signal-box. Joe Murphy leans from the open window and salutes. The driver and stoker salute back. On we go, past the siding, past the creamery, under Augaboura Bridge. The brakes squeal again and the train grates heavily to a halt. My father climbs down and I follow him, carefully.

'Thanks,' he says.

The driver and stoker wave and we step off the permanent way, onto the grass. The train moves, the flat wagons juddering and pushing against each other. They pick up speed. The whistle sounds. The train fades down the line to Maganey. My father watches it out of sight and then we turn and walk back along the track, the few hundred yards to the car.

'That's the last steam train through here,' my father says. 'I thought it'd be nice for you to be able to say you were on it.'

We get into the car and drive through the town, to meet my mother, and he never mentions that afternoon again.

forty-seven

He believes he's turning his life around, particularly where the children are concerned. There may be other friendships he's betraying but he's determined not to surrender the ground he has made with the children.

His father and he are talking more. His father has taken to calling occasionally to the cottage. The coldness of the house is a constant in his conversation.

'You need to keep a good fire going. Always keep it going, no matter what, and let the last hour be the hardest.'

The children are the other constant but he never brings up the subject of separation. The old man is making a huge effort not to go beyond his concern for the children and their welfare, trying to care without interfering.

His father's intentions are the best but there's still something that keeps them from being at ease in each other's company, some gap that has never narrowed, much less closed. John's recollection keeps cutting across his father's purpose. He can go for weeks and months without letting the childhood memories loose and then, out of nowhere, they arrive of their own accord, dragging ill will in their wake.

Another argument is over. The house breathes uneasily. His father is sleeping heavily. His mother wakes him.

We're getting out of this place.

It's two o'clock in the morning. She dresses the boy and they pack a couple of changes of clothes in a case and walk down through the village. And the ten-year-old boy listens and advises and begs that they go back *until morning* because neither of them can think of anywhere to go. He wishes there were somewhere, he wishes they could get on a train and start a new life. He'd willingly leave his toys and his room and his friends and everything and everyone that's familiar if it brought an end to the endless warfare. So, they walk slowly around by the River Road and back by the Square and, finally, home again.

The boy wakes another time and finds that his mother really has left without him. He's eleven years old and his father has been drinking heavily for several weeks.

He dresses in the dark. The kitchen clock says ten past two. He lets himself out the back door and, for some reason, intuition perhaps or fear, he doesn't go through the village. Instead, he walks down the garden, out over the back fence and across the football field. He has no torch but there's some moonlight. He catches sight of his mother standing at the gate between the football pitch and Keatley's field, close to the ditch at the bottom of their old house on the Low Terrace. He goes and stands beside her. For a long time she says nothing, but when she does speak she's crying.

What am I going to do? she asks.

I don't know. Will you come home?

For what? What is there to go home to? Is this going to go on forever?

I'd like you to come home, he says.

He's in tears himself. She's never left without him before.

They stand for ages in the field and, in the end, she turns and starts walking towards the house. He follows, afraid she may disappear if he goes ahead. When they get into the house they rekindle the fire and make tea and sit and talk and even laugh about his father. He notices that her legs are muddy, she must have fallen in the field. He tells her he'll talk to his father, he'll try to make him see sense. But he doesn't. He's eleven years old and he can't find any words that make it possible to talk man-to-man with his father.

The following Sunday evening, while his parents are sitting downstairs in grey silence, he takes an abstinence pin from his mother's coat and pins it on the lapel of his father's railway uniform jacket. It's meant not so much as a gesture of great consequence as simply a way of telling his father what he can't say to his face.

He wakes in fear the next morning at the thought of what he has done, thinking there'll be war, but to his amazement his father doesn't mention the pin.

That evening, his mother takes him aside.

You didn't have to do that, she says. *It isn't always the way to do things.*

But she's smiling.

That night, as they sit watching television, his parents hold hands, something he has never seen them do before. They laugh a lot and whisper sometimes and he knows they're happy now and he's tempted to trust in the future but he can't.

All John knows, in these years afterwards, even after his mother's death, is that he owns acres of resentment and he can't let go of them. What he doesn't have is the vision to see enough of his father in himself to reach some understanding of why he himself is the way he is. Neither does he have the largeness of heart to accept the gestures his father is making. The old man's good intentions are no match for his son's bad memories. He knows, if he were to look carefully, that he'd see what he dismisses as weakness is, in fact, both a generosity and a paternal indulgence that he refuses to acknowledge.

And he realises that there's no reason to suppose his children will be any more impressed by his own good intentions when faced with their own store of memories. Memories of a man on the verge, a man screaming, a man out of control, a man whose anger terrified them, a man who wanted to put his arms around them and hold them safe from everything, but a man who couldn't save them from himself.

forty-eight

We're fighting, my father and I, we fight whenever we can. This time it's about politics. Sometimes the fights are just sparring. Just to keep in practise. Just in case we get too close and begin to believe the peace will last. But this is a serious argument, one that comes from the heart.

I'm twenty-one, in my last year in college and I'm out on bail, having been arrested for picketing the home of the Taoiseach, in protest against the introduction of the Offences Against the State Act, a bill I see as oppressive and anti-democratic. It's 1974 and the island of Ireland is in a state of tension. I'm out on bail, my father is an Independent politician with Government sympathies.

When we're arrested, several dozen of us, we're charged and held in the Bridewell in Dublin. I wake at four in the morning to the sound of someone playing the "Red River Valley" on a harmonica. I smile at the wan, haunting sound, even though I don't feel like smiling. The following afternoon we appear in court. We expect a ticking-off and the Probation Act. Instead, we're sentenced to a month in jail. Our solicitor appeals and we're given bail. My sister puts up the money for me. Two weeks later I go home for the weekend and walk into an ambush. My mother is quiet but makes it clear that she's not impressed. My father is less circumspect.

'What the bloody hell do you want getting yourself mixed up with that crowd for?'

'It's an unjust law.'

He refuses point-blank to get dragged into the political niceties.

'You're a bloody fool if you put that class of thing before your career. What happens if you land in jail when your exams come up in May? What happens when you have a record?'

'And what about all the stuff you told me about yourself when you were young? You were in *Fianna Eireann*.'

'That was different, that was nearly sixty years ago.'

'Why was it different — because that was you and this is me? You're the very one that gives out about things but when I do something you're up in arms. And, at least I'm not trying to kill anyone.'

'Don't be smart with me.'

He's angry and I'm elated.

'These bastards you're in with wouldn't know what republicanism was if it stood up and bit them.'

'You'd know, wouldn't you?'

'Yes I would. They're nothing but bloody communists. I saw them in my time, they infiltrate a union and stir things up, then leave you high and dry, out on a picket line without a bob in your pocket. I'd know them all right. Trouble-makers that'll do you no good.'

'It's not about them, it's my own decision.'

'Easily led,' he snipes, 'easily led and soft in the head. Wait till you're trying to get a job with a criminal record behind you. See then where it goes, when you're out of work.'

'Well I won't be living off you, anyway. I wouldn't want to be.'

He ignores this but his eyes darken and I know I've hit the mark. I press on.

'I won't spend my time sitting on a barstool talking about what should be done; I'll get off my arse and go out and do it, no matter what you think. I'll do what I believe, so just get off my back.'

'You're an impudent pup.'

'Yeah, yeah, yeah,' I turn away.

A week later my aunt dies and I come home for the funeral. Afterwards, my father and my uncle, who's a retired policeman, corner me in the pub and the argument begins all over again.

'You're in deep water,' my uncle says.

'I don't think so.'

'Fellow travellers, money from Moscow, not a great start for a young fellow setting out in life.'

'At least they're not Blueshirts,' I take a swipe at his own politics.

My father cuts in.

'Don't be such a smart aleck, now.'

'The laugh will be on the other side of your puss if this sticks, I can tell you,' my uncle says, his face flushed and angry. 'You'll have the Special Branch on your heels wherever you go. Nowhere to run, nowhere to hide and no one to run to.'

That night, at home, my father tries to mend fences.

'I rang about the case,' he says, naming a local man

who's a Government Minister, 'to see if he could be of any help. He says there's nothing he can do.'

I explode.

'You had no right to do that. This is my case. I did what I did because I wanted to do it. I'll take responsibility for own actions. I'm old enough to decide what I want for myself. I don't want you asking favours off the very people I'm protesting against or anyone else for that matter. You had no right, absolutely no right to do that.'

'Let me tell you, you could be glad of any help in the long run. Or would you rather end up behind bars?'

'Yes, I would.'

'Well we'd soon hear a different tune if you did.'

'Says who?'

'Says I!'

'What you say counts for nothing with me.'

'Well, maybe you'd be better off if it did, if you listened to sense rather than listening to some of the people who have your ear.'

'Meaning?'

'Meaning whatever you like!'

'Well, I bloody don't think so,' I say and I'm shouting.

'Mind your blood pressure,' my father says sarcastically, 'mind your blood pressure or you'll have a stroke.'

The slamming door echoes behind me.

In the end, our case comes up and we get off, no jail. I sit my final exams and qualify and come back home to teach, back to live in my parents' house. The rows go on about socialism, about music, about unions, about football, about nationalism, about anything we can find to differ over.

forty-nine

His wife and he are sitting on the bonnet of the car outside her house. The sun is shining and the children are across the street, playing with their friends.

'Things are going all right,' his wife says.

'I suppose they are.'

'Are you happy?'

'Happier than I was a year ago.'

'Happier than you were ten years ago?'

He doesn't answer for a while.

'You know the bit in the *Our Father*?'

She looks at him as though he's lost his mind.

'Which bit would that be?'

'The bit that says: *'Give us this day our daily bread and forgive us our trespasses as we forgive those that trespass against us.'*

'Yeah.'

'Well, it's like that. There's this day and the way I'm feeling now. And there were those days and the way I was feeling then. I'm sorry for all the things that went wrong in between. I try not to compare. I can't.'

'Neither can I.'

'But I am sorry about all the crap in between.'

She nods and shrugs her shoulders. Their son flies by on his bicycle, their daughter and her friend giving chase. They come from the shadows of falling leaves, into the light and melt into the shadows again.

'They seem happy.'

'They are.'

Later, as he's about to leave, his wife says: 'There's the other bit in the *Our Father.*'

'Which bit?'

'The bit that says: *'And lead us not into temptation.'*'

He looks at her and she's laughing and then she becomes serious again.

'The thing is,' she says, 'neither one of us set out to make life miserable for the other and, for a long time, we made things work pretty well. For a long time we were happy. And I can't say I'm unhappy now. Can you?'

He shakes his head.

'That's not bad then, is it? That's not a bad way to be. When you think about it, we've been in worse places.'

As he drives away, the children are laughing. He tells himself their laughter is genuine, they're content with the way things are and their contentment is contagious. He feels gratitude and excitement in equal measure. The trick, he knows, is to maintain this feeling.

fifty

I've been teaching in Castledermot for a couple of months. This is a small village and there are few places to go and little to do. I've made friends with a couple of the younger teachers, and I'm involved in the local theatre group, but village social life is less than exhilarating for a single twenty-two-year-old. And then I remember a woman who grew up with me. I have no idea why she comes into my head but here she is. I haven't seen or spoken to her in four or five years. I don't even know where she works, but I decide I'm going to find her and ask her out.

It takes me a week to pluck up the courage to walk into her aunt's shop and casually enquire as to her where-abouts. Her aunt tells me she's in Dublin.

'I thought I might give her a ring,' I say. 'Just to catch up on old times.'

'Of course.'

'You know, just to say hello.'

'Why not,' she says, a smile playing on her lips.

'Yeah, I might.'

'You should.'

'Do you think so?'

'If you want to.'

'Right. I will.'

'Do.'

I stand at one side of the counter. She stands at the other. I nod. She looks at me. Suddenly I remember that this is a shop and the woman has been really helpful.

'I'll … ah … I'll take a packet of Kimberley biscuits … please.'

'You don't have to buy something. The information was free.'

'No … yes … no, I wanted them. I came in for them. Yeah.'

I pay for the biscuits.

'I have the phone number here if you want it. It's a work number. You'll normally get her there after nine at night.'

'Thanks.'

I leave with the precious number scribbled on the back of a brown paper bag. I go home and write it into my diary and into my notebook and into my school diary. I don't want to mislay it. I don't want to have to ask for it again.

It takes me another two days to summon up the courage to ring. I don't dare call from home. I don't want my parents in the background, listening to my every word. I drive to Carlow and sit in the car, watching the clock tick past nine.

Give it till twenty past.

I count out the change for the call and then count it again. Getting out of the car, I see a woman step into the phone-box. Fifteen minutes later she finishes her call.

She smiles as she steps out again, holding the door for me, leaving me with a receiver that reeks of perfume. I dial the number and then hang up because I'm sure I've missed a digit. I try again. A voice on the other end. I ask for the woman by name.

'Just a minute. I think she may be in another department tonight.'

Bugger.

'No, hold on. She's here.'

The soft sound of footsteps on linoleum.

'Hello.'

'Hi. This is John MacKenna. I'm sorry for ringing you out of the blue like this. I got your number from your aunt.'

'Yes.'

'Ahm, I just thought I'd give you a ring, you know. I was wondering if we could meet … just for a chat, for a drink or a coffee or something. Just, you know, if you were free. If you're not it's OK. I mean there's no problem I won't be … I know this is a bolt out of the blue.'

She's polite. She could tell me to shut up and stop rambling. Instead, she says: 'That'd be nice. I'm working lates this week but I'll be home next week. We could meet then.'

'Really?'

'Sure.'

'Brilliant.'

'I'll be home on Wednesday morning. Ring me at home, Wednesday afternoon.'

'Great. Right. Yeah. I will. Thanks.'

I wait for her to hang up and then I throw the receiver in the air and catch it on the way down. I whoop and, turning to leave the box, am faced with three people waiting to use the phone. One smiles, one glowers, one looks embarrassed for me, but I don't care.

In the car I put on a tape of *Rubber Soul* and fast forward to track nine.

Ah girl and then that inspired *fffff*, that intake of breath that says everything there is to say.

Ah girl, girl …

We go out that Wednesday night. I collect her from her home. The family sheepdog comes barking across the yard to meet me. We drive to Carlow and sit in a quiet pub and talk and talk. About growing up, about work, about life, about hope. When I drop her back home I ask her if she'd like to go out again.

'Sure. When?'

'Tomorrow night?'

'Yeah.'

'What would you like to do?'

'We could go to the pictures.'

And that's what we do and, afterwards, we go for a drink and when I drop her home the sheepdog comes barking across the yard again.

'I really enjoyed tonight,' she says.

'So did I, would you like to go out again?'

'Yes, I would.'

'Tomorrow night?'

She nods and we both laugh.

'Do you want to come up to my house, listen to some music or something?'

She says nothing.

'We don't have to, we could do something else, whatever you like.'

'It's just that, well, your mother was my teacher.'

Enough said.

'Tell you what. I'll collect you at eight. We'll decide then.'

The following night we drive and walk and drive and talk and the hours fly by and I think I could happily live my days like this for the rest of my life.

We arrange to go to a dance the following night. And I go home and lie in bed and the curtains are open and the moon is sloping over Rice's Hill like a vagabond and the football field is washed in its yellow brightness and the garden trellis of dying roses splinters the sallow warmth.

And I lie there wishing I'd telephoned this girl months ago and then I'm glad I didn't because I wouldn't be falling in love like this, now, if I had done. The sweet uncertainty would be over. Instead of lying awake while the night pulls its rug of stars across the sky, I'd be sleeping. Instead of getting up with all the energy of a three-hour sleep, I'd be dragging myself out to face another working day.

The following evening the sheepdog doesn't bark.

'I think he's getting to know your car,' she says and my heart leaps.

We drive to the Rugby Club in Carlow and we dance and we laugh and we talk and I want to kiss her but I don't. And the band plays the last slow song and I don't want it to end but it does because the last song always ends. And we're driving home through Knocknagee and Prumplestown and down the side of Barn Hill and turning onto the narrow road between the Green and Mullarney and all my words are falling behind me like rusty, broken leaves.

Only when we reach the gate of the girl's house and park the car do I face the inevitable. There won't be a tomorrow night; she'll be back in Dublin; her working life will go on; our lives will break in different directions. Falling in love for four days isn't falling in love for life.

Through the car window I can see the form of the sleeping sheepdog curled outside her door.

'What time are you going back to Dublin?'

'After lunch.'

I nod.

'I've really enjoyed this week,' she says quietly.

'Have you?'

'Yes, I have.'

We're silent for a couple of seconds. The dawn of Sunday morning is edging over the hill that shelters her house.

'I really wanted to kiss you earlier,' I say.

Refracted light from the new day catches the side of her face. She looks pale and even more beautiful.

'If I had kissed you, what would you have done?'

She smiles warmly.

'I'd have responded,' she says.

'I'm glad,' I say because I believe her. But we don't kiss.

Driving home, with the sun already fingering the trees on Fraughan Hill, I open the car windows and turn the tape volume up and let the morning breeze blow the Beatles away.

fifty-one

Christmas is coming. He's determined to make this a happy and joyful season. He thinks about the word *Advent* and all its meanings. Arrival, appearance, entrance, lighting. He will find a reason to celebrate each meaning.

He cuts a tree. This year, he's decided, there'll be none of the plain, unadorned simplicity of last year. The red bows are there but so are the newly bought baubles and lights. He puts holly on the mantelpiece and over the doors. He puts candles in the windows, back and front.

He takes the children to Dublin and they dawdle in Grafton Street, enjoying the lights and the shop windows. They go from shop to shop, no rush. They're three children. He takes his time in choosing presents, he spends more than he should and feels no guilt. Back home, he puts Christmas carols on the CD player and they sing along with them, raucously, tunelessly on his part, and they laugh about their efforts. He rediscovers the meaning of happiness.

fifty-two

'It's not like we're spoiled for choice,' Joe Whelan says.

Here we are two suave, eighteen-year-old college boys home for the holidays and Castledermot is proving a great disappointment in Christmas week. We're standing at the end of the School Lane. The choices are stark, a night of TV or a night of carol singing on the village streets.

'You've some class of a voice. I've none. So, if I'm prepared to make a fool of myself,' Joe asks, 'why can't you do the same?'

'Right,' I say, 'we'll give it a shot.'

Joining the choir in the freezing church, we hug the radiators that are colder than the frost lying on the fields. Jigging, we listen to the late-comers hurrying across the gravelled yard outside. We share a sheet of carols, familiar songs we've sung at home and in school concerts, songs whose melodies rise like a spring inside us and soften our tuneless tune. Joe and I are two-thirds of the male section. The choir mistress listens patiently.

'Sing as if you could,' she smiles. 'Or just rattle the tins.'

Outside the church, we light the lanterns and walk to Farrelly's, at the end of the street. Our rising voices are strengthened by the familiarity of the carols that reverberate as far as the sleeping singers in Coltstown graveyard.

Carolling our way from door to door, from pub to pub, the tins grow heavier.

Standing on the flagged floors in Doyle's, we sing to the worn faces of countrymen who listen as though the music matters. They'll hum these carols later, cycling home the desolate roads to Mullaghcreelan or Fraughan Hill or Ballyvass. And they'll remember our voices and in them the voices of the lost, the absent and the dead. Whatever they give in charity is given back in memory.

There are other faces on the street, lonely faces at open doors; rapt faces at windows; small children peeping through frosted upstairs curtains.

Along the cottages in Woodlands, there are darkened yards and snarling dogs until the smiling faces appear and the dogs are hushed. Or is it the same dog, racing ahead of us from yard to yard? Each voice calls *Shep* and each dog falls silent at the name.

We sing on the Square and the shadows slowly give up the unexpected figures of men who appear like the ghosts of Christmas past, before melting again into the dark. On we go, along the street, the lanterns guttering and weeping but never going out. On past the final streetlights, to one of the last houses in the village.

The choir stands at the gate while Joe and I crunch across the frozen grass, drawn by the lights of a Christmas tree in the shining hall. I ring the doorbell. Joe kicks his boots against the frosty gravel. We wait. Slowly the door opens and a vision appears. A girl we've known all our lives, not well because she prays in a different church and went away to boarding school, but a girl we know nonetheless. And here she stands, fair hair in a shimmering wash about her face. She wears a long pink dress and her eyes catch the light from the Christmas tree beside her. Behind us the choir is singing 'Oh Holy Night' but I hardly hear our motley group. Instead, the words and music surge as if angels are singing. I know, if I look, I'll see the same dozen choristers in the lantern light at the gate but I dare not look for fear of missing the girl.

She smiles and goes inside to get some money and then she's back, stepping into the yard, dropping the coins into the tin.

'Happy Christmas,' she says

'Happy Christmas,' I stammer and I mean it.

I wish, how I wish, I were the young man escorting her to the Christmas party in Athy or Carlow or wherever she's going. I am envious but I am joyous, too. I'm in the presence of beauty and even now, even in my naïveté, I suspect this moment, this night, this music will be with me for the rest of my life.

As the carol ends, I hear feet on gravel and realise Joe is already halfway down the avenue. I smile and the girl smiles back and then I'm retreating. At the gate, I stop and look again. She's still standing at the door, the tree lights forming an aura about her, the cherry blossom of her dress resting on her shoulders, her hair a deeper golden than before.

Above me the stars sputter and burn. I glance again but she's gone, leaving only the light from the tree to sprawl across the hard white lawn.

'Come on,' Joe says quietly, 'there's Skenagun to do.'

And so there is.

Returning, half-an-hour later, the gates to the girl's house lie open. There are tyre tracks in the perfect frost.

fifty-three

It's Christmas week. He has three visitors to the cottage, arriving like Magi who got separated on the long journey. Three more than he had last year.

Noel Lambe, his friend and neighbour, is standing formally in the doorway.

'I was thinking,' he says. 'It's a lonely time around Christmas. If you feel like it, if things get you down, there's a room in our house. You'd be very welcome. You can stay as long as you like. You won't be disturbed. There's only Tommy and myself there. You'd be most welcome. I just wanted to say that.'

It's late and the back door swings open and Ned Kerr blusters in from the black wet night. His coat soaked, his hair plastered down by wind and rain.

'Jasus, there's a wind out there that'd blow a tinker off his wife.'

He unbuttons his coat, throws it onto a chair and pushes the kettle onto the ring of the Aga.

'Well, what denture-cracking delicacies have you made this week?'

'I baked and iced two Christmas cakes.'

'Hiroshima and Nagasaki!'

John cuts one of the cakes. Ned tastes it.

'Well it's lost that concrete consistency you had last year. You'd miss that.'

'Will you have another slice?'

'I will.'

And he does and a third.

The conversation turns to the past, to growing up, to teenage, to embarrassment.

They swap stories.

Later, when the house is quiet and the fire is dying, John remembers a summer night in the early Seventies.

He's part of a group who run a mobile disco, four of them hawking last month's records around the country in a Mini. They're doing a tennis-club hop that night in Bagenalstown and he's dancing with a girl he's fancied for weeks. She tells him her name is Eleanor and, after the last dance, after the lights have been dimmed and Nilsson has sung 'Without You', he asks if he can leave her home and is stunned when she says yes.

They walk through the town. Neither one speaks.

He wants desperately to say something that will touch her but inside his head he's singing the line from Gallagher and Lyle's 'Sparrow': *When Eleanor sings in the choir, it's like a lark in summer.*

It's one o'clock on a balmy summer morning, tatters of daylight still fluttering in the west — yesterday's and today's.

The streets are theirs, deserted, wide and warm.

'Do you sing?'

'What?'

'Are you a good singer?'

She looks at him, smiles, shrugs her shoulders.

They walk on through a silence that he doesn't want to break. And then they're standing under a tree outside her house. He'd love to put his arm around her, to tell her how unbelievably beautiful she is with the street light trickling like honey through the leaves. He wants to kiss her but he's afraid. Instead, he starts talking about Vincent Van Gogh, telling her about the painting *Wheatfield with Crows*. Talking and talking, wishing he could shut himself up. And Eleanor stands there, politely listening. He goes on for fifteen minutes, until the other three arrive in the Mini, hanging out the windows, blowing the horn, making smart remarks, and he knows he has to go.

He turns, quickly, and mutters: 'Goodnight, my dear,' and as the words stumble from his mouth he could shoot himself. He's twenty, she must be seventeen, and here he is sounding like some daft old codger, three times her age. Jesus, talk about making a fool of himself. He scrambles into the back seat of the car and pretends it never happened.

The last thing he sees through the rear window is this beautiful girl standing in the streetlight at her garden gate, a look of disbelief – if not disdain – on her face.

He never goes back to another disco in the town.

His father is the last of the Magi to arrive and he, too, eats the cake. He even stays for a second pot of tea. This truly is becoming a season of good will.

'Did you ever think of going into politics?'

John shakes his head.

239

'You used to be very interested, when I was involved.'

'I got disillusioned. Age and family responsibility.'

'I always thought you'd end up going into politics.'

His father is silent for a moment.

'Do you remember the red flag, when I left Fine Gael and went Labour?' he asks.

John nods and laughs, remembering a Sunday morning as they drove to Mass.

On the village Square, beside his father's election posters, someone had hung a jacket, turned inside out, with a placard reading *Turncoat* beside it. And above the placard hung a red flag.

'Well, we know where that came from,' his father had said, getting out of the car and taking down the placard, coat and flag.

Later, he had burned the coat and placard and put the rolled-up flag in the rafters of the garage.

In the end, victory was sweet.

One spring evening, years later, when John was appearing in a local production of *The Risen People*, his father had taken the flag down and given it to him to use as a prop, enjoying the irony, knowing the very people who had hung it in the Square in the first place would be in the audience.

'So no politics for you?'

'Not now.'

'Maybe just as well, it takes up a hell of a lot of your time.'

He finishes his tea and stands up. John helps him on with his coat and carries the presents to the car. As he's about to drive away, his father rolls down the window and hands him an envelope.

'That's a card to put on your mantelpiece. I thought there mightn't be too many cards there but I see you did all right.'

'Always room for one more,' John says. 'Thanks and happy Christmas.'

'Happy Christmas.'

Back inside, he opens the envelope and takes out the card. A ten-pound note flitters to the floor.

fifty-four

How to describe the indescribable promise of light in the corner of the window, edging beneath the curtain. I look across at the other bed in our room, the lads' room. My brother is fast asleep. I slip into the frosty air and follow the wedge of brightness from the landing light. Down the stairs, stopping on the bend, waiting, listening.

What if he's still there? What if I go down into the hall and open the sitting-room door and he's still there, taking the presents from the sack? What if he turns to face me, the slice of cake that I left for him half-in and half-out of his mouth? What if the glass of lemonade is raised to his lips as I poke my head around the door?

I sit listening on the stairs for a few minutes, trying to ignore the breathing of the sleepers above, tuning my ears to the silence below. No sound!

I've no idea what time it is but I venture on, across the hall, turning the squeaky knob on the sitting-room door, pause, push and step after it into the light of the Christmas tree. And there they are, Santa's presents on the floor beside the grate, and beside them the empty glass and the plate with its relics of crumb. Year in, year out, these are what fascinate me most, these crumbs that have fallen from Santa's lips. To be so close to his presence, to touch the glass and the plate that he touched, as close to the dream as the dreamer can come.

And, afterwards, there are the toys and the books and the sweets. I eat and play and read and eat and play and fall asleep on the couch and, when I wake again, it's daylight and someone has put a blanket over me and the fire is lighting and I can hear the family, busy in the kitchen.

This is Christmas Day. *Christus natus est!*

fifty-five

He gets off the afternoon train in Athy station and stands, watching the engine and the carriages shuffle under Aughaboura bridge, away to Carlow and onward to Waterford. And then he's alone on the platform and in the falling darkness he notices the signal-cabin lights, sees the signalman moving about up there.

And he remembers coming off another train, sometime in the early Seventies, arriving home for the Christmas holidays, and going up to the cabin. Sitting beside the blazing turf fire while below him his father, then a man in his sixties, shunting pole in hand, lifts the heavy chains between the goods wagons on the siding.

And afterwards his father comes up the wooden stairs, winking at him and saying: 'Won't be long now.'

He sees him pulling back the stiff and shining levers, his big hands wrapped round them, snapping the release handle. The signal falls at the railway bridge, the points lock and the way is open for the goods train to move on.

He watches him stand on the top step of the cabin, penknife in hand, paring a pencil, the wood chips flying through the winter air.

And he remembers, as they walked to the Austin A40, his father tossing the keys to him and saying: 'You might as well drive, the practice'll do you no harm.'

fifty-six

Christmas dinner is over, the washing up is done. The afternoon is an intermission between the feast and the opening of the family presents. Boyhood Christmas afternoons were spent playing with the toys Santa had brought, but these teenage afternoons are spent walking the dogs.

First there's the negotiation of the footpaths with their humming bicycle wheels, whirring pram wheels, whizzing skate wheels, ricocheting footballs and racing children.

But beyond that, and beyond the ragged hedges that have here and there saved a leaf from the autumn storms, there's the open space of the football field, the Little Hill, Joe Shea's bridge and the Rocks.

As I grow older, this is the most wonderful time of the day. The feeling of goodwill, the anticipation of the presents still piled under the tree, the thought of the Christmas tea and the cutting of the Christmas cake and, afterwards, a session of cards.

Out here, in the empty fields, I'm part of the shadows that rise and sway with the fog swelling off the river. The dogs blindly scour the riverbank, and at the far end of

Rice's Hill, an early fox sets off about his scavenging. I wish him well. Tomorrow will be too late. Tomorrow the Christmas spirit will evaporate and the fox will be running for his life.

fifty-seven

It's the second week of January and the snow has come, as it often does, too late for Christmas, but just in time to extend the school holidays. It falls like the snow in his memory and he wakes to find himself a prisoner in the cottage. Travelling to work is out of the question. He battles to the garage for kindling and gets the range and the open fires in the sitting room and bedroom going. The house sings with spluttering timber. He makes a huge pot of soup and bakes bread and does some work on a short story. In the afternoon the children ring. They tell him they've been off school and they want to go tobogganing on Mullaghcreelan and he promises he'll get them out to the cottage if it's humanly possible.

'It won't be today. I can't get the car out.'

'Tomorrow then?'

'If I can at all.'

He sets out walking on the empty road. There are no tyre marks in the clean snow. To his right, three snow-bound fields away, an enormous bare-branched sycamore towers above the whiteness. The rise and fold of the fields hides the hedges but wherever the land dips the black branches of hawthorn and alder spike the powdery ground. He wants to walk to that tree, to reach it against the odds of wind-packed snowdrifts and splintered hedges and bitter coldness blowing in from the east.

Climbing a gate, he sets off across the first field, plodding, lifting his feet heavily and letting them fall back into the deep, soft snow.

At the end of that field, he finds a gateway in the hedge and hoists himself up onto the bars and sits, lord of all whiteness, getting his breath back. The glare of the snow is dazzling, even under a dull and overcast sky. Taking a deep breath, he sets out again, trying to follow the lie of the land, to avoid the deeper drifts. Pushing on, through an opening in another hedge, the tree now fifty yards ahead of him. He walks, head bent, eyes half-closed against the wind coming in from his left. And then he's there, in the heavy shelter of the sycamore, its branches bending beneath the weight of the snowfall.

On his way back, it begins to snow again and the wind lifts the falling flakes and whips them into his face. Head down, he keeps his eyes on his footprints and retraces his steps, back to where he started from. Sliding onto the roadway, he leans against the gate, exhausted and elated.

He drives to Athy to collect the children. There are two sets of tyre tracks in the frozen snow and driving is a matter of getting into one and staying in it until he reaches the town. The journey takes more than an hour each way but they spend the late afternoon tobogganing down the side of Mullaghcreelan on plastic sacks, dodging between the trees, their runs lit only by light reflected from the snow. They have the hill to themselves.

Their shouts ring through the empty forest like the voices of the first, or last, of humanity.

As they ramble home at six o'clock, the church bell is ringing in Castledermot. It's the first time he's heard it from Hallahoise but, this evening, its chimes carry through the cold air, across the clean snow to the yard of the cottage.

fifty-eight

Dina Whelan rings the Angelus, twice a day, every day. At midday and six o'clock in the evening the sound of the bell peals across the village and, if the weather is right, out into the fields beyond the huddled houses.

Joe Whelan and myself know when the bell is due, long before the rest of the village hears it. Dina Whelan lives on the Low Terrace and we see her leave her house and cut across the church field at the foot of the road. We wait at the gap in the ditch, knowing she has to pass through it to get to the church on time.

'Can we come with you, Mrs Whelan?'

'Not today, maybe another day. Your mothers wouldn't know where you were.'

'We could run up and tell them.'

'Then I'd be late.'

She's always polite, always softly spoken, never short with our endless enquiries.

'We could ring it for you.'

'You can. Another day.'

We have this vision of swinging from the long rope, rising into the air like puppets, the heavy tongue clanging above us, hammering against the metal helmet of the bell, its discordant music rolling out across the gardens, music that is of our making. We could be the ones to call the parish to order; stop the farmers in their tracks; freeze the coal men in mid-lift; lock the awkwardly balanced guard, cap in hand, to his bicycle; keep the Canon praying for as long as we wanted. We could swing together and in turns until the village ran out of prayers or we ran out of devilment.

We live in hope of the day when Dina Whelan comes to us with some story of a sore arm or a sick child or an emergency that outweighs the heavy tolling of the Angelus bell. And we'll say, *Yes, yes, we know, of course we know. Eighteen rings. Certainly we'll ring it for you.*

But she's never sick and we're never called upon. Winter and summer, in sunshine and in rain, even that winter when the drifts are four-feet-deep across the church field and she has to go the long way round, the Angelus rings at twelve and six.

Years afterwards, as an altar boy, I do get my chance to ring that heavy bell. Tolling the old people in and out for the last time, ringing the slow reminders of tragedy, swinging the freestyle on Sunday mornings to alert Massgoers to the half- and quarter-hours.

Over the years, I ring for funerals and weddings and Masses and Benediction. I ring the dramatic bells of Easter and the celebratory bells of Christmas but I never ring the Angelus.

fifty-nine

February has come. For a couple of days the weather is mild and the hedges put out a few, tentative buds, but then the wind changes and there's frost, followed by a driving rain that smashes like gravel against the window panes. The light of Christmas and the radiance of the snow that followed are forgotten and winter makes a late churning on the mucky paths and in the flooded dykes.

He digs even deeper to keep his equilibrium. It isn't just the weather. Changes of weather simply mean the fields and the wood and the riverbank wear a different set of clothes. There are still places to walk and the contrasting pleasures of walking them when a gale howls or when the sun strips fifteen minutes of blue from the greyness of the sky. He'd be happier without the greyness and the incessant slanting of the rain across the garden but they don't drag him down. It's something inside, some weight, like a dead dog in a sack, which keeps pulling him back to where he's been.

He's well into writing the collection of short-stories. *A year of our lives* it's called. The rawness inside him and the shallowness of the graves he thought he'd safely dug for his feelings constantly surprise him. And yet he feels an obligation to go on. There's nothing else about which he feels the same absolute need to write. There are other notions in his head but that's all they are, bits and pieces of ideas. The stories he's working on are burning to be written. They are cuts that need examination and cleaning and bandaging. He can feel them tearing him as he writes and yet he can't ignore them. Sitting at the typewriter is like performing surgery on himself without an anaesthetic but he needs to do it to survive.

So as the writing goes on, he does the things he always does when he's despondent. He walks a lot. He works hard. He keeps his nose to the grindstone of what has to be done. He ignores all thoughts of freedom or gladness or delight.

When he needs the memory of light and brightness, he looks at a photograph of the wide limbs and heavy flowers of the laburnum tree that bloomed in summer outside the window of the house that he has left. Even in the photograph, the blossoms hang in heavy fists of yellow and the bits of sky that peep through the leaves are a deep, summer blue.

The laburnum photograph is one of a dozen or so that he taped to the side of the kitchen dresser a month after he moved into the cottage. There are shots of the children, together and separately. His daughter in the snow, his son in his buggy; both of them, hamming it up, at the seaside. There's one of his brother, sister and himself on a swing in the garden in the Low Terrace. These are his antidotes.

What surprises and disappoints him, most of all, is the way in which melancholy has bided its time, sat out the autumn and Christmas seasons, smiling cynically while he went on in the mistaken belief that he had beaten it.

So he counts the used condoms in the forest car park on his Monday morning runs. He sticks to his writing. He searches for a light for the darkness inside his head and sometimes he finds it and sometimes he doesn't. And some of the time he understands the expression his father uses for drunkenness – *in the horrors* – because the horrors of uncertainty and grief and rage continue to ensnare him.

Sometimes, in desperation, he abandons his writing and spends days and nights walking the woods and the fields or leafing through a box of old photographs or reading poems.

His isolation reminds him that, in spite of a year-and-a-half of seclusion, things are not quite back to normal. He's not automatically on anyone's visiting or mailing list. In some ways, nothing has changed. He still sits up at the sound of a car in the yard, guessing which of his half-dozen callers it might be. He still falls easily into the trap of hiding from the world.

Mostly, he believes, he's satisfied with his own company, but when the cards or callers come, especially the unexpected ones, he knows there's more to life than solitude.

He tells himself he should make more phone calls, get out, drive somewhere, visit someone, see a film, do something. But he never does. Mustering the energy to shake off the shadows is more than he can manage.

He loves the days when the postman drops something other than an electricity or phone bill through the letterbox. There are a couple of postcards that have arrived at the cottage over the past eighteen months, missives that were sent with light hearts and arrived like prizes. Those cards hang with the photographs on the dresser, part of his arsenal for holding things together and keeping darkness at bay. From time to time, he takes them down, turns them over and reads the words that speak of sunlight and thoughtfulness and true friendship.

The days are lengthening. His publisher has accepted *A year of our lives*. He's working in the garden again. He tells himself that if he can just hold on until the summer sunlight, he'll be all right.

At the end of February, on her anniversary, he visits his mother's grave in Coltstown, a cemetery on the side of a hill, overlooking the Lerr valley and across to the hill at Knockpatrick. The graves are surrounded by apple and cherry and laburnum trees.

This afternoon, the place is deserted. The wind is cold but the day is dry and he leaves some flowers at the foot of his mother's headstone. Wandering, he visits the graves of people he knew well. His next-door neighbours, O'Connell's, who bought the plot next to his parents. Peter Murphy, in the top-right-hand corner. Aylmer's, inside the gate. Mena Hickey, who was their next-door neighbour on the Low Terrace.

In the new section, he visits the graves of young people he taught, men and women who died on the doorstep of adulthood. And here they are and here are their stories. Killed in road accidents, dying in childbirth, taking their own lives.

He thinks about Liam Dunne, a childhood friend and classmate. One of the gentlest boys in Castledermot school, always grinning, never pushing to be the hard man of the playground. When they were nine, Liam became ill and was missing from school. His classmates assumed he'd caught a cold or the measles but he didn't come back.

And then John's parents started taking him to visit Liam, out to his house, perched on a hillside, looking steeply down onto the village.

The last time he saw Liam was on a Sunday at the end of August, 1962. It was a warm afternoon and the boys were together in Liam's bedroom. They were working their way through a box of Milk Tray and reading comics. Their parents were in the kitchen, having tea. The boys could hear the low hum of adult voices.

Liam's face was pale, as it always was those days, but he was still smiling, still laughing. And then he started to be sick and John ran to call his mother, thinking his friend was about to die.

He was kept in the kitchen for a long time. When he went back in, a warm breeze was blowing through the open bedroom window. Liam was lying quietly in bed, his head on a white pillowcase, his face even paler than it had been before. He was still smiling, but he seemed to have lost all energy.

'He's going to sleep for a while,' his mother said. 'You can come and see him during the week.'

'All right,' John said.

He could hear the bees in the garden.

'You take these — they'll only make him sick again.'

She handed him the half-full box of chocolates.

'No, it's all right, thanks,' he refused, though, deep down, he wanted to take them.

'Take them,' Liam said and he did.

Liam's mother left the room.

'I'll come up and see you during the week.'

Liam smiled and nodded.

'See you then.'

'See you.'

He never did see him again, for Liam was too ill by the following week for visitors and he died in early September.

The night of Liam's burial, John's mother came up to his room.

'There's nothing to be afraid of you know,' she said. 'Liam was very sick. He's gone to heaven.'

'I know that.'

'If you have any bad dreams or anything, just call your dad or myself.'

'All right.'

'Would you like the light left on in your room?'

'No, it's all right.'

'You're sure?'

'Yes.'

'Tell you what, I'll leave it on till we're going to bed, is that OK?'

'Yes.'

He wasn't afraid of Liam Dunne's ghost, how could he be? How could anyone feel threatened by the laughing boy who kept on laughing right to the end?

Some time afterwards his mother gave him a memoriam card. It had a photograph of Liam, his face lit up in that broad grin that John always looked for in the school yard. Underneath it read:

In Loving Memory of
Liam Dunne
Plunketstown
Castledermot, Co. Kildare
who died on
September 4th 1962
Aged 9 years. R.I.P.

On the other page of the card was a verse.

The bud the gardener gave us,
A pure and lovely child,
He gave it to our keeping,
To cherish undefiled.
But just as it was opening
To the glory of the day,
Down came the Heavenly Father
And took the bud away.

John didn't fully understand the verse, he thought it was about the roses in his own parents' garden, but he was glad to have it. It was the first time anyone had given him a memoriam card. His mother's prayer book and his father's wallet were crammed with them, but this was for him, this was his. He kept the card on the locker by his bedside and he prayed for Liam Dunne every night.

sixty

Sometimes, on dark evenings in November or January, as I pass the old graveyard, on my way to Mahon's for the milk, the dead gather to watch me. These same dead, who ignore me in the long summer afternoons I spend tracing their names and dates on the crumbling headstones, dawdle now in the shadows of the church, their eyes glinting as I run past the closed gates, the empty milk can clattering against my short-trousered knees.

Ten minutes later, when I step out of the light of Mahon's dairy and onto the black lane, they move down to the wall, peering over it, knowing I can't run with a full can of milk. Their collected breath is a mist in the frosty air, their sighs a nervous grumble in the stripped branches above me. I swear then that I will never set foot inside the graveyard again. Only let me get to the sanctuary of the weak light pooled outside Doyle's pub door and I'll never disturb them again with my searching and reading ever.

But in the wet murk of winter Saturdays or the bladed sunshine of summer days I do come back, concocting their stories, listening for one voice, one solitary whisper.

Why?

Not because I believe this old graveyard is any more special than a hundred others scattered about the countryside but because it is mine. It talks to me about my people, my history, my life lived through the folk memory of countless lost labourers and farmers and shopkeepers and monks and children and ruined young women. That place, that small field around the old church, those hummocks and headstones and crosses and graves, webbed and snared by the fingers of ancient trees, all these are my roots too.

Whatever I fear on dark nights is the very same thing that lures and intrigues me when there's any kind of light across the ancient and recent graves. If the newly dead are my acquaintances and friends, their ancient sleeping neighbours must be too. This thought makes me happy.

When they whisper after my frightened figure, the words I hear are: *This is our place, this is where we belong and this is where you belong, too.*

And, when I hear them, I stop being afraid of the darkness that has nothing to do with their lives.

sixty-one

There's a phrase that keeps coming into his head: *an accessory after the fact*.

A lot of the time, that's how he feels, that he's living his life after the facts, that he reacts to things rather than knowing where he's going.

Doubt swamps him. He turns his back for a minute and it comes crashing, lifting him off his feet. But then the waves of darkness are followed in turn by waves of light. Sometimes he can see no way of ever letting go of what he was, still technically is, husband, father. He wants to be a man who looks after his family, but he can't extricate himself from that other part of being a family man, the part that doesn't work, the part he's spent two years trying to clarify. He wants to believe he can still be a father, a good father, without saying that everything that has happened in the last two years is a lie or a game.

He and his wife visit a counsellor. The woman listens to what they say. She listens to them separately and together. She asks questions, she notes the answers and asks the same questions again, or slightly different questions that throw up answers overflowing with anger and sadness and regret and suspicion.

They come out of the sessions mentally fatigued, physically weary, totally confused.

They see her again and again. She asks to see the children. She talks to the four of them together. One of the last things they do as a family is sit and talk to this woman about how they will live their lives now that they no longer are a family.

She asks them to come back, just the two of them. She talks to them together and then individually. More questions, more clarification. Hour by hour, emotions are broken down and examined and put back together, or more or less together, again.

Some days they wonder if this is all worthwhile. Some days it seems to make sense. Some days one or the other of them is positive about the outcome. Most days they just don't know.

And then, one afternoon, when the counsellor says she feels they need to let go, John feels an enormous sense of relief, a sense that someone outside the choking world of his own head believes *that the best thing, the healthiest thing, the most positive thing they, as a couple, can do is to let go.*

'You can never be separate in the sense of two people walking away and never turning back because the children are your children and you will always be their parents. You'll always be family in that sense. But, as individuals, you have to allow each other to move on. I think you've already achieved that. But you have to allow yourselves to move on, too. There's no sense in beating yourselves up about what has and hasn't happened. That won't do the children any good and it certainly won't contribute to your physical or mental well-being. The only thing it will do is make your life more painful and more difficult and that's in no one's interest.'

They drive home from Dublin together.

'In spite of all the talk with the counsellor, we don't talk about the past, do we?'

'No. It's hard to talk after those sessions. I'm just always exhausted. You?'

'The same.'

'It isn't that the past wasn't important, isn't important. It's just a hard place to go back to at the minute.'

'I know that.'

'Do you think there'll be a time when we can go back?'

'Maybe. Maybe it's not a good place to go.'

'Maybe not.'

A long silence.

'When she said we should let go, get on with our lives, how did you feel?'

He wants to be convinced.

'Relieved. And you?'

'Relieved as well.'

'That's good then.'

'Yes.'

So much talk and so much left unsaid.

sixty-two

My final year in college.

For months I've been clinging to this love affair, refusing to let it go, refusing to accept the gentle way out that's being offered. In the end, the woman sits down with me on a low wall near her bus stop and says what I should have already heard before she said it.

'I don't love you.'

After the bus has left, after she's gone, I feel as if I'm choking. I walk among the suburban trees and cry for myself.

Months later, when I have the courage to think about that afternoon, I hope I'll never hear those words again and hope I'll never have to say them.

sixty-three

He busies himself with house hunting. He scours the local paper week by week, he gets to know every estate agent in a twenty-mile radius on first-name terms. Whenever he drives anywhere, he ends up reversing into gateways to view *a property with potential*. Anything, no matter how old or derelict, that rises more than two feet above ground level has *potential*. He spends afternoons and weekends visiting houses. He grows accustomed to the smell of percolating coffee and learns to associate it with the smothered, darker smell of damp.

The houses he loves he can't afford. The houses he can afford are either in God-forsaken spots, rat-infested, or are *unique*—which generally means he could pump into them the rest of his life's earnings and still not cure the rising damp, the dry rot, the sagging roofs.

Sometimes the search depresses him and sometimes it amuses him. Sometimes the lingo of the auctioneers intrigues him and sometimes it simply annoys, but he knows that he needs to find a house by the summer's end and spring is already plunging through the fields and ditches all around him.

The alternative to a house is a flat and, after two years in the countryside, the thought of an apartment above a noisy street holds no appeal. And he also wants a garden.

Easter is around the corner; the evenings are lengthening; something will turn up; it has to.

sixty-four

It's a Holy Week in the mid-Seventies. There's bitter weather for the time of year. It's getting dark and I'm climbing Mullaghcreelan Hill, as I do every Holy Thursday.

Dies irae.

The forest passage forms a perfect corridor in the last glow of evening. I follow the little light that remains up the slippy, rising ground. In the clearing there's the deserted cottage, glanced by moonlight, and then on I go, along the slithering mud of that day's sleet.

And after he had said all this, Jesus left with his disciples and crossed the Kedron Valley. There was a garden there and he went into it with his disciples.

I'm out onto the space at the summit of the hill and the stars are scattered leaves on the tops of the silent trees. And then the silence is smashed by the flacking of a pigeon's wings. Below me and across the valley the lights of houses flicker. The wind whips up clouds like torn garments, throwing them in the face of the moon.

Now it was cold and the servants and the guards had lit a charcoal fire and were standing there warming themselves; so Peter stood there too, warming himself with the others.

Driving back, I slow the car on the Square in Castledermot and, through the open door of a pub, I see old men gulping pints, Black Friday is coming, twenty-four hours of closed pub doors. And I catch a glimpse of a young woman I know, fighting hard to keep her man, and already I know the story. She'll cling to him, accept everything he says and does until she loses him in marrying.

At home, a daffodil has opened fully on the lawn. I examine it in the headlights of the car and look across the fields, back to the black bulk of Mullaghcreelan Hill with the moon slanting over it.

Again Peter denied it and at once the cock crew.

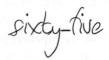

sixty-five

This second spring at the cottage brings good weather and the promise of a settled summer. There are vegetables in the garden. He has put a lot more work into them, laying out the small patch in neat rows of potatoes, cabbage, lettuce, scallions, beans and peas. The sight of all this orderly growth resurrects memories of how the place looked the first time he saw it, as a child, when the Wilkies had it at its best.

An intense early heat has the flowers running riot on the roadside. Primroses are flooding down the inclines of the banks. Where the violets were sparse last year, they are now clumped between the huge roots of the oaks and sycamores.

And Easter brings its own particular drama, as it always has done.

Holy Thursday night. He reads the passage about the Last Supper and, afterwards, climbs the still, warm flank of Mullaghcreelan, up through the trees that are already budding. At the summit, the night air is calm and mild and the moon is already perched high above the Wicklow Hills.

Good Friday afternoon. He's working in a church in Graiguenamanagh, Co Kilkenny. The choir sings and the words of the Passion cut sharply into the lazy sunlight that drifts through the clear windows of the white-washed medieval building. The sky outside is great and blue, and the unseasonably warm weather adds a certain irony to the dark history of the day. Driving home, the countryside is electric with growth and colour.

The children come to the cottage every weekend and they live, more or less, outdoors. Sunday afternoons are spent in the garden, playing games of football and tennis and hide-and-seek. The radio in the open back window provides an unobtrusive soundtrack of football commentaries and results. The casual horror of Ayrton Senna's death in the Formula 1 race on May Day in San Marino stills their laughter but it seems there's nothing the world can throw at them that can entirely spoil the pleasure of summer.

Now there are acres of bluebells on the back of Mullaghcreelan Hill. Woodbine climbs out over ditches and drops into the dry, dusty dykes. Crab-apple trees blossom along the roadside near the humpbacked bridge. June opens its windows and, day after day, the sun drenches the cottage inside and out.

July brings, out of the blue, news that a friend is selling her cottage, twenty miles from Hallahoise. He meets her, they agree a price and the deal is done. No auctioneers, no haggling. He'll move in August. It's all as simple as that.

He's living out the last sunny weeks in Hallahoise, convinced that this is finally the time to accept that he has recovered from guilt and depression and uncertainty. He tells himself he never really sank at all, rather he dealt with the end of his marriage with incredible fortitude and poise. Everything is all right now. Two years on, he's on the edge of a brave new world.

July is staining the yellow fields with poppies and he's drifting through the summer in the bright belief that he has found the peace and well-being that has eluded him all his life.

It's Sunday afternoon, he's packing his books in boxes and the children are tidying the garage. Suddenly, a stone of absolute terror and melancholy falls on him out of the clear sky. He's petrified at the thought of moving. It isn't the financial commitment that worries him, but rather the absence of any emotional assurance. He knows he should have some sense of satisfaction but he doesn't. He's distraught at the idea of leaving here, terrified by the responsibility he's undertaking. His energy drains. He can't see beyond the things that he has to do. He's faced with the realisation that he doesn't know a sinner in the town-land to which he's moving. He's going twenty miles, but it might as well be a thousand. He's panic-stricken and all the anger and worry and apprehension that were rolled up and put away in the previous months come tumbling out and swamp him. He feels sick and shocked. He wants to run from everything but there's nowhere to run.

The children come, laughing into the house.

'For Christ's sake, do you have to come in like screaming lunatics?'

He's screaming himself.

They stop dead in their tracks, the old uncertainty returning to their faces, betraying the fact that it's never been very far away.

'Why can't you behave like normal children? Can you not see I'm up to my eyes.'

They left him laughing twenty minutes ago, happily piling books on the floor, now here he is, eyes blazing, brow furrowed, shouting at them for nothing, searching for the slightest excuse to be angry.

'For fuck's sake, can I not get anything done without you coming in on top of me.'

'We just wanted to tell you we put all the stuff in the garage in boxes. It's all ready for you, ready for the car.'

This is more than he had asked or expected.

'Right,' he says, gracelessly. 'Great.'

'We'll just go back and make sure it's still OK,' his daughter says quietly.

Her brother is standing behind her. Their eyes are wary, and they're anxious to be away from him. Yet again, he wants to put his arms around them, hug them, pile them into the car, drive them to Castledermot and buy ice-cream cones, enjoy this summer afternoon. Yet again, he doesn't. He's too petrified. Frightened by the future and by the past that has suddenly reappeared, uninvited.

The children go back to the garage. He watches them through the window, sitting on the neatly packed boxes, aimlessly kicking stones. Always watching through windows, always too far away and too late.

'Fuck, fuck, fuck, am I going to be like this all my life?'

That evening, after the children have gone back to their mother, he drives to Prumplestown Mill, and parks the car and walks along the banks of the River Lerr. He needs to get away from the cottage and the boxes, bags and cases. He wants to recover some of the peace that has come into his life in the past few months.

Somehow, he hopes, returning to a childhood haunt, getting away from the mayhem of moving, will put his mind at rest, reassure him that he's not slipping into the waters of uncertainty.

Above the mill, the river is quiet. Willow and dog-rose dip their leaves in the slow waters. It's hard to believe there's any movement on the river at all. An evening half-way through July and the trout are slapping in the shaded stream. Corn throws shadows on the crumpled headland. Woodbine lifts in the warm breeze, drinking in the last deep heat from the day. The granite wall of the mill rises out of the race. A water hen glides easily between the banks and bows into the overhang. The sun rests a moment on the grass where the river narrows and deepens.

A mound of poppies pokes from a load of gravel, an abandoned trailer above them – rust, red and grey. Midges flock between the bushes and the faded yellow heads of parched and scattered iris.

The sun goes down and he can smell the night river-smell as the moon rises silently above the fields of corn and grazing cattle.

Everything is beautiful, everything idyllic but it's only a hiding place from the way things are, back there in the rest of his life. He can't stay out here forever. Sooner or later he has to go back to the cottage, finish his packing and face the facts. He's moving. He has bought a house.

Everything is new, apart from the bleak terror of disillusion, which clings to him like an incurable disease. He loves the quiet of the evening and the splendour of the river and the majesty of the deserted mill, but he despises them too because their beauty has no power to mend.

These last days in Hallahoise Cottage are strange. He hates leaving the place. In his two years here the house has become a home to him, not just a place to live. He's leaving, as he came, at a time when the fields are vibrant with yellow rape and crimson poppies and golden brown wheat. The bearded barley hangs over the headlands in heavy promise.

He's leaving certainty, a place where he feels grounded, for a place he hardly knows at all, a house he has visited regularly, but in a part of the county that's far removed from the roads and lanes on which he grew up.

He came to Hallahoise alone and uncertain but sustained by the comfort of a familiar landscape. Where he's going there's a different kind of responsibility and none of that familiarity. John Clare would be proud of his dithering.

sixty-six

It's the end of a long wet summer. Some crops are in and some are lodged. Hay lies in the fields, cut and soaked. Word comes to the village of a small farmer in the outlying part of the parish, a man with a handful of acres, a man we knew to see at Mass on Sundays. He's been found hanging in the shed he called his barn.

In his empty kitchen, beside his dinner plate, is a note that reads: *I turned this hay seven times, I can turn it no more.*

sixty-seven

It has taken him a week to leave Hallahoise Cottage. He
has travelled back and forth in the evenings, after work,
filling the car with boxes and bags and unloading them at
the other end, storing them in his new home. But every
night he comes back to Hallahoise and sleeps there, reluc-
tant to be let go.

Mullaghcreelan Hill has never been greener or richer
or more inviting.

He doesn't trust himself to walk up through the trees.
It's enough to see them in passing, enough to remember
that he ran and walked and lolled away the hours up there.
Enough to remember that he stood naked at the summit.
Enough to acknowledge how much comfort he found
among those trees. Enough to recall the smell of the late
evening bluebells.

The countryside has never looked more beautiful or
more abundant or more inviting. Already, the crab-apple
trees are weighed down with fleshy fruit.

In the farm lane, the tractors come and go. The harvest
is in full swing all around him, combine-harvesters
lumber day and night through fields that are flaxen in the
morning and a stubbled, reddened brown by nightfall.

sixty-eight

'That's great,' my father says.

We're driving up Mullaghcreelan Hill in the Morris Minor. The ditches are snowed over with Mayflowers, the sun is shining and we're on our way home from Athy. I'm sitting on the edge of the hot, leather passenger-seat, leaning across to hold the big wheel, steering the car.

'That's great. Hold her steady now.'

To my left, through a gap in the ditch, I see a man leading two huge plough horses across a field.

'Keep your eyes on the road, nice and steady now.'

We breast the hill and I steer down past Bushfield farm. At Lambe's corner my father takes the wheel again.

'We'll make a driver of you yet.'

sixty-nine

It's his last afternoon in the cottage. He checks the rooms. Nothing remains. The floors are washed and dried. The cooker sits in the corner of the kitchen. The bed is stripped. In the sitting room, the couch and armchairs stand with their backs to the wall. The empty bookshelves dip in the middle. The sturdier food shelves in the pantry, which he didn't build, are bare and straight. The house is ready for giving back.

He locks the back door and walks down past the blank walls of the garage, gets into his car and drives up the lane to return the keys.

He makes the usual conversation with the owner, talks about moving and decorating and the like, but he just wants to be on his way; he doesn't have the heart for chat. Driving out, he takes the main avenue to avoid passing the cottage. He feels some sense of excitement at the prospect of his first night in his new home but he also feels a great, deep sadness.

seventy

A country hall, music playing, late sun blazing through cracks in the blacked-out windows. A girl in an ankle-length dress, a girl whose hair leapt and settled and leapt again in the dazzling, dancing air, a girl who was beautiful, who was waiting for me.

And when we danced her perfume was a kiss on the mouth. And that kiss, those kisses when they came, took away my uncertainty and confusion. We were in love and the things we whispered were secret and impulsive and urgent. We were in love, too much in love not to say it.

seventy-one

It's a Saturday afternoon. John has been living in the new house for six months and the children and he are lying in the straw in the barn loft, laughing so hard that they're unaware of the car in the yard. Only when they stop to draw breath do they hear the engine start again. John hurries down the ladder and into the yard. His father is about to reverse back out onto the lane. John races after him, tapping on the car window. His father smiles, signals and drives back in.

'I thought the place was empty,' he says. 'I saw your car there but I thought you might be off rambling.'

The children come from the shadows of the barn.

'Well, look who it is,' John's father says and he hugs them.

Inside, while the kettle sings on the range, John shows his father round. It's his first time in the new house.

'It's a lovely place. How old is it?'

'Hundred and twenty years.'

'Well-built.'

'Yes.'

'Do ye like it?'

The children chorus *Yes*, gabbling to tell him about their rooms, about the garden, about the barn and the loose boxes and the orchard they've planted and the places to play hide-and-seek and the slide they made when the lane froze.

'Ye're all doing well then.'

'All doing really well,' John says. 'No arguments.'

'No fighting,' the children grin.

'No arguments and no fighting is a good thing.'

Back in the kitchen, while John wets the tea, his father searches in his pocket and produces two bars of chocolate for the children.

'And I have a house-warming present for you,' he says.

He hands John a brown paper bag. Inside is a rusted cigarette tin and inside that is the small plastic racing driver, The Green Man.

'I was planting a tree at the top of the lawn and I dug it up. I thought you'd like to have it. You should tell this pair about it, it's the kind of thing they should know. It's been buried for forty-six years.'

'Tell us,' the children say.

And he does.

seventy-two

There are these two people who work together, let's say, in a radio station. They know each other but not too well. The woman has a little boy. The man has two children, a girl and a boy. He gives her a present of a book for her son's first birthday. It's a book about a bird. They talk now and then. He's going through a bad time.

A year later and I'm sitting with her in the radio station canteen. We sit for an hour, talking. I tell her about my new house, about the things I'm doing in the garden, about how well I'm settling there. She should be back at work but she's waiting for me to say something. She knows, by the way I've broken the handle off my teacup, that I have something to say, but I say nothing. Finally, as she rises to go, I mumble: 'I was, ah, wondering, if you might, you know, like to go out to lunch some day, if you like, no pressure or anything, no harm done if you don't. You know, if you like. Anyway …'

She thinks I'll never stop talking.

'I'd love to.'

'Would you?'

I'm genuinely surprised.

'Yes.'

'When?'

'Tomorrow or is that too soon?'

'No, no, that's great.'

epilogue

John is standing at his parents' grave. It's a summer morning. When he came to the grave the night before, to clean it and put flowers on it for the annual blessing, everything was intact. But now he finds that half the plot has subsided and one side of the gravel is several inches below the level of the other.

The cemetery is still quiet apart from the occasional figure bending by a headstone or kneeling to arrange flowers. He tries to rake the gravel with his foot.

'Waste of time,' his father's voice murmurs at his shoulder.

'I'm just trying.'

'I wouldn't worry about it. The lid caved in. Five years, that's not bad.'

'It would happen today.'

His father laughs.

'Let the last hour be the hardest.'

'I'll get a couple of bags of gravel tomorrow. Level it up.'

'Good enough. Did you marry the Frenchwoman?'

'She's not French. She's from the Aran Islands.'

'Offshore, anyway,' his father laughs again. 'How are the children?'

'They're well, very well.'

'And you, how's your life?'

'I'm fine. A lot more content than I used to be.'

'Contentment is a good thing.'

'And you?' John asks. 'How are things with you?'

'I'm flying. This place is filling up.'

John glances across the cemetery. People are streaming through the gate and making for their family graves.

'That's not what I meant,' his father laughs.

'Of course.'

A moment of silence.

'How are the spuds coming?'

'Very well.'

'No blight?'

'No, I kept them sprayed.'

'That's the style. I think I'll make a bee-line out of here,' his father coughs. 'I was never very comfortable with this class of thing. And you won't forget the gravel; your mother likes it kept spick and span.'

'I won't forget.'

'Good man.'

'I'll talk to you again?' The statement comes out as a question.

'There's no point in looking over your shoulder all the time,' his father laughs again. 'You just end up walking into walls.'

And then the laughter is gone, and someone calls his name, and he sees his sister crossing the sun-lit cemetery towards him, smiling, and he waves.